Oxford School Shakespeare

Richard II

Edited by

Roma Gill, OBE
M.A. *Cantab.*, B. Litt. *Oxon*

Oxford University Press

Oxford University Press, Great Clarendon Street, Oxford OX2 6DP

Oxford New York
Athens Auckland Bangkok Bogota
Buenos Aires Calcutta Cape Town Chennai Dar es Salaam Delhi
Florence Hong Kong Istanbul Karachi
Kuala Lumpur Madrid Melbourne
Mexico City Mumbai Nairobi Paris São Paulo Singapore
Taipei Tokyo Toronto Warsaw

and associated companies in
Berlin Ibadan

Oxford is a trade mark of Oxford University Press

© Oxford University Press 1998

ISBN 0 19 832003 5 (Schools edition)   1 3 5 7 9 10 8 6 4 2
ISBN 0 19 832004 3 (Trade edition)   1 3 5 7 9 10 8 6 4 2

Illustrations by Martin Cottam

Cover photograph by Donald Cooper shows Jeremy Irons as Richard in
the Royal Shakespeare Company's 1986 production of *Richard II*.

For Anastasia

Oxford School Shakespeare
edited by Roma Gill

Typeset by Herb Bowes Graphics, Oxford
Printed in Great Britain at the University Press, Cambridge

Contents

Crisis in the Monarchy

The king of England is a unique personage, holding the highest office in the land. He has not achieved this position by effort or intelligence; he has not won it by force and conquest; and he was not elected by the people who are his subjects. He was *born* to be king—chosen by God for that special purpose. The king is 'God's substitute, His deputy anointed in His sight' (*1*, 2, 37–8), and he rules by Divine Right. His position is inviolable: he cannot be dismissed, discharged, or deposed:

> The breath of worldly men cannot depose
> The deputy elected by the Lord. (*3*, 2, 56–7)

Such, at least, was the theory . . . Successive governments found it convenient for the right hierarchical ordering of society, and monarchs—most especially Richard II and Elizabeth I—were (understandably) its most passionate supporters. The Elizabethans forming Shakespeare's first audiences were taught the doctrine in their churches, their schools—and even in their theatres!

But even Richard II knew that theory and practice often diverged, and that there were (*3*, 2, 156–60) many 'sad stories of the death of kings' telling how some had been deposed, slain in war, haunted by ghosts, poisoned by their wives, killed when they were sleeping—'All murdered'!

The body of the king was sacrosanct, anointed and consecrated in the service of Almighty God and his country. The great position conferred great privileges and made equally great demands, and a monarch who was not to abuse the one or shirk the other needed to be possessed of supreme self-control. But the monarch was also a normal human being, a man or woman with human needs and desires—

> I live with bread like you, feel want,
> Taste grief, need friends. (*3*, 2, 175–6)

—and also with human frailties. And human nature, especially human weakness, will almost always triumph over human theory when these are at odds.

Richard of Bordeaux, grandson of Edward III, ascended the English throne when he was only ten years old and, disciplined by his uncles, gave promise of a glorious future when he outfaced the rebels of the Peasants' Revolt in 1381. But twelve years later he declared 'I am of full age to govern my house and my household'. There followed a career of wilful and irresponsible extravagance, which soon precipitated a political and constitutional crisis. In 1399 he consented to abdicate his throne in favour of his cousin, Henry Bullingbrook.

Not much more than two hundred years later England was again faced with a potential crisis in the monarchy. Like Richard II, Queen Elizabeth was childless, surrounded by influential favourites, and with no apparent heir. She obstinately refused to nominate her successor, and senior statesmen so feared threats to depose her that, during her lifetime, all editions of Shakespeare's *Richard II* were published without the central deposition scene (*4*, 1, 154–317). The play was performed, nevertheless, in the public theatres and, most probably, in an uncensored version. When the Earl of Essex (who was indirectly descended from the Duke of Gloucester) attempted to seize the crown in 1601, his supporters arranged for a private performance on the night before their abortive coup. For this they paid an extra £2 to Shakespeare's acting company, who argued that there would be small audience for such an old play.

Family tree

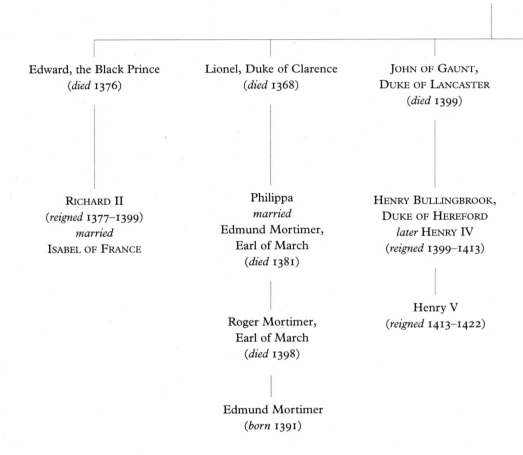

King Edward III
(*reigned* 1327–1377)

Edward, the Black Prince
(*died* 1376)

Lionel, Duke of Clarence
(*died* 1368)

JOHN OF GAUNT,
DUKE OF LANCASTER
(*died* 1399)

RICHARD II
(*reigned* 1377–1399)
married
ISABEL OF FRANCE

Philippa
married
Edmund Mortimer,
Earl of March
(*died* 1381)

HENRY BULLINGBROOK,
DUKE OF HEREFORD
later HENRY IV
(*reigned* 1399–1413)

Roger Mortimer,
Earl of March
(*died* 1398)

Henry V
(*reigned* 1413–1422)

Edmund Mortimer
(*born* 1391)

EDMUND LANGLEY,
DUKE OF YORK
(*died* 1402)
married
DUCHESS OF YORK

Thomas Woodstock,
Duke of Gloucester
(*died* 1397)
married
DUCHESS OF GLOUCESTER
(*died* 1399)

Two sons,
died in infancy

EDWARD,
EARL OF RUTLAND
DUKE OF AUMERLE
(*died* 1415)

Leading Characters in the Play

Richard II Richard of Bordeaux, born 1367, reigned 1377–99. His early promise of courage turned into wilful extravagance and autocracy, and he was generally held responsible for the death of his uncle, the Duke of Gloucester (Thomas of Woodstock). Richard believes that he rules by Divine Right, inherited through descent from his grandfather Edward III and confirmed by his coronation and anointing in Westminster Abbey. The events of the play cover the last two years of his reign, during which he moves from triumph to disaster and from tyranny to near-heroic tragedy.

The Queen A French princess who has a close and loving relationship with her husband. Shakespeare's character (who is not given a name in the play) is more like Richard's first wife, Anne, to whom he had been deeply devoted. Richard's second wife, Isabel, was not ten years old when the events of the play took place.

John of Gaunt Duke of Lancaster, fourth son of Edward III. 58 years old in 1397, he is profoundly patriotic and unswervingly loyal to the king—although he is well aware of Richard's part in the murder of the Duke of Gloucester.

Henry Bullingbrook Duke of Hereford (Herford), son of John of Gaunt. Exiled because of his challenge to Mowbray, he returns to claim the rights of his inheritance. When Richard resigns the crown, Bullingbrook becomes King Henry IV.

Duke of York (Edmund Langley), fifth son of Edward III. Although he is critical of Richard's actions, he is left in charge of the kingdom during the king's absence in Ireland.

Thomas Mowbray Duke of Norfolk. He had been in charge of the garrison at Calais when Gloucester was imprisoned there, and was instrumental in Gloucester's death.

Duke of Aumerle As Earl of Rutland (son of the Duke of York) he had been created duke by Richard and was one of the king's most devoted supporters. Holinshed says that 'there was no man in the land to whom Richard was so beholden as to the Duke of Aumerle; for he was the man that, to fulfil his mind, had set him in hand with all that was done against the said duke [of Gloucester]'.

Bishop of Carlisle A supporter of King Richard, Carlisle articulates the orthodox position on the subject of the abdication or deposition of a monarch (*4*, 1, 115–49).

Synopsis

Act 1

Scene 1   King Richard hears Bullingbrook accuse Mowbray of the murder of Gloucester.

Scene 2   The Duchess of Gloucester demands revenge for the death of her husband.

Scene 3   Bullingbrook and Mowbray prepare to fight but their duel is stopped by the king. Richard pronounces sentences of exile.

Scene 4   Richard hears that Bullingbrook has left the kingdom—and that Gaunt is sick.

Act 2

Scene 1   Gaunt, dying, laments the state of the nation. Richard seizes his subject's estates and departs for Ireland, leaving York in charge. Northumberland has news of Bullingbrook.

Scene 2   The queen remains in England with Bushy, Bagot, and Green. The news is worrying, and York is confused.

Scene 3   Bullingbrook travels south, winning friends and collecting allies. York gives him hospitality.

Scene 4   The Welsh soldiers desert Richard.

Act 3

Scene 1   Bullingbrook executes Bushy and Green.

Scene 2   Richard reaches Wales—but his followers are defecting.

Scene 3   Bullingbrook demands his rights—and Richard surrenders the crown.

Scene 4   The queen, walking in the garden, overhears a discussion of the state of the nation.

Act 4

Scene 1   Another dispute: Bullingbrook listens to Bagot and Aumerle. Richard deposes himself. Westminster hatches a plot.

Act 5

Richard II: commentary

Act 1

Scene 1   After the ceremony of a royal procession, the play immediately plunges its audience into the heart of a quarrel. The accuser, Bullingbrook, speaks succinctly, with well-chosen words and rhyming couplets whose strong endings seem to enact the deeds they describe. The passionate speech of Mowbray, the defendant, is less controlled. Although despising the 'bitter clamour of two eager tongues', he is ready to engage in a war of words and explanations so that the quarrel can be fully understood.

    The charge is misappropriation of funds, conspiracy, treason, and murder, and Bullingbrook's accusation reaches rhetorical heights with an invocation of biblical precedent—the blood of Abel crying to the heavens for vengeance (1, 1, 104–5n)—and the triple rhyme of 'chastisement . . . descent . . . spent'. But the king is unimpressed—'How high a pitch his resolution soars'—and promises an impartial hearing to Mowbray. His anger now under control, Mowbray defends himself, admitting one little fault (for which he has, he claims, been duly forgiven) but denying the major crime of murder and returning back on Bullingbrook the charge of treason. King Richard attempts to take the heat out of the situation with a little joke, but tempers are roused and honours have been challenged.

    Trial by combat—a fight to the death—must now determine the outcome of the quarrel. 'Justice' will ensure that truth will triumph!

    Up to this point Shakespeare has given the audience no help in judging the situation—although some of his contemporaries would have learned from the chronicles that the Duke of Gloucester, Thomas of Woodstock, died at Calais whilst in the custody of Mowbray. Holinshed, Shakespeare's main source, goes still further, saying that 'The King sent unto Thomas Mowbray . . . to make the Duke secretly away'.

Scene 2   This scene, devised by Shakespeare, clarifies some of the issues that have been raised, and contrasts different attitudes to the murder of Woodstock. John of Gaunt recommends Christian patience—but the Duchess of Gloucester demands revenge with a passion that increases as the scene proceeds. The verse reflects her temper: she measures her words into couplets as she regains self-control, but emotion breaks through into blank verse. Taking leave of Gaunt, she must return to the ruined, empty house which is now the emblem of her life.

Scene 3   From private grief to public spectacle. A long scene, moving effortlessly between blank verse and rhyming couplets, presents an occasion of great splendour. Holinshed describes a three-day event to which all the dukes came 'in great array, accompanied with the lords and gentlemen of their lineages [and] the king caused a sumptuous scaffold or theatre and royal lists there to be erected and prepared'. The ceremony, however, disguised the brutal reality of a contest which could be expected to end in the death of at least one of the combatants. Before fighting, both must swear that his cause is just—but since one of them must be lying, he will commit perjury and be deservedly overthrown!

The audience is now in the position of a privileged spectator. Having heard the exchange between Gaunt and the Duchess of Gloucester, we are better able to understand and evaluate the characters and proceedings—Mowbray, eagerly zealous, going to battle 'as jocund as to jest'; Bullingbrook, more sober in his confidence, taking 'ceremonious leave' of the king, his friends, and father; and King Richard, cautious in his apparent impartiality. The scene is building to a climax with the arming of the contestants, the final declarations, and the command to the trumpeters when the king—inexplicably—calls a halt to the proceedings.

The '*long flourish*' allows time for the king's conference with the dukes—a two-hour session, according to Holinshed—and then the king announces Council's decision. The adversaries are both sentenced to exile, but the sentences are not equal. Bullingbrook accepts his punishment with uncharacteristic patience, but Mowbray is surprised and outraged to find himself condemned to 'speechless death' in life-long exile. Pronouncing Mowbray's sentence 'with some unwillingness', the king had seemed to acknowledge some truth in the claim that he was financially in debt to Mowbray (*I*, I, 129–30), and now Mowbray hints that the obligation is even greater and deserves some 'dearer merit'. Despite the eloquence of the appeal, Richard must now be adamant and

Mowbray must obey—but not without a word of warning to the king.

When Mowbray has departed, Richard demonstrates another aspect of royal power by reducing the sentence on Bullingbrook. The altercation with Gaunt brings into focus the strengths and limitations of power and language, and language is further questioned when Gaunt attempts to reconcile Bullingbrook to the king's decree. But words are no real comfort for genuine distress.

Scene 4 Richard at last reveals himself, relaxed among his friends, in the slighting reference to 'high Herford'. The verse takes on a conversational tone as they discuss Bullingbrook's departure. Richard has plans to raise money for the wars in Ireland by means of the infamous 'blank charters', and news of the sickness of John of Gaunt is welcomed as being another possible source of income. The king can now be seen for the tyrant he really is.

Act 2

Scene 1 On his death-bed, John of Gaunt feels himself newly inspired—literally! He finds breath enough to articulate the most damning criticisms of the king and his government. A loyal patriot, Gaunt is anguished to know that 'this sceptred isle' is being so abused, betrayed, and bankrupted by a monarch who is deaf to all good counsel. Sickness drives him to desperate word-play when Richard appears, and Gaunt makes wild puns on his own name and state of health. The king is unsympathetic and uncomprehending, but Gaunt's passion cannot be restrained. He accuses Richard of having disgraced himself and dishonoured his heritage, reducing the king (who should be above the law) to the level of a subject. Richard's threat with its reference to 'the royal blood' provokes still more recrimination, and Gaunt charges Richard directly with the murder of Gloucester.

The sick man leaves the stage and York makes a feeble attempt to pacify the outraged king, but soon news is brought that Gaunt is dead. Richard now makes the biggest mistake of his career: he commandeers all the 'plate, coin, revenues, and moveables' belonging to Gaunt to finance his wars in Ireland.

York's patience can bear no more. Recalling the wrongs done to himself, his family, and the kingdom, and invoking a comparison with Richard's father, the elder statesman spells out to the king the full implications of what he is doing. The confiscation of Gaunt's estate, depriving Bullingbrook of his inheritance, is a violation of the time-honoured laws of 'sequence and succession' which have brought Richard himself to the throne of England. But the king will not hear, and, creating York 'lord governor of England', sets out for Ireland.

The remaining lords, speechless until now, voice their disgust at what has been done to Bullingbrook but are inclined not to blame Richard himself so much as those who are his advisers: 'The king is not himself, but basely led By flatterers'. They detail more of the extortionate taxes and other iniquitous devices being used to bleed money from common people and nobles alike. The situation begins to sound desperate—but Northumberland (having made sure that he speaks to sympathetic ears) imparts the latest news from the north: Bullingbrook has landed in England and is attracting supporters and forces as he moves towards the south.

Another long scene, covering the events of several weeks, has shown the king's fortunes beginning to crumble. Superbly powerful and confident in his visitation of Gaunt, he has alienated the affections of his uncles, the most important of his country's nobility, the hearts of the common people—and even the respect of the audience.

Scene 2   One person, however, remains true to Richard—his wife, whose distress at Richard's going into Ireland cannot be comforted by the sophisticated fancies of Bushy's wit. Her emotion is unfeigned and her fear becomes infectious as the situation worsens. Her 'nameless woe' soon finds a name: Bullingbrook! Troubles follow fast upon each other in 'a tide of woes' until the company collapses into bewildered confusion with the Duke of York, who has found that 'everything is left at six and seven'—his son absent, his sister-in-law dead, the Household dispersed, and no money for the wars that will surely ensue. With loyalties torn between duty to the monarch and recognition of the injury done to his kinsman, York bustles away—leaving Bushy, Bagot, and Green to make a quick appraisal of their own positions. With very little hope for the future, they make their escapes in different directions.

Scene 3   Bullingbrook's fortunes improve as Richard's deteriorate. Marching down from the north, accompanied by an obsequious Northumberland, he draws supporters like a magnet. The scene travels fast, moving across the English countryside until Bullingbrook reaches Berkeley, where he encounters the first opposition—which is easily overcome. The confrontation with York is perhaps the turning-point of the play. York is impatient, not waiting for his messenger—Berkeley—to return, and very conscious of his role as the king's deputy. He speaks out for the right and for the defence of the realm and monarchy: Bullingbrook has come to claim his rights, in conflict with the will of the monarch. His argument has the firm foundation of precedent:

> If that my cousin king be king in England
> It must be granted I am Duke of Lancaster.

Northumberland acknowledges the force of this, Ross and Willoughby are of the same opinion, and York himself is sensitive to Bullingbrook's wrongs. But York is emphatic that two wrongs do not make a right: 'To find out right with wrong? It may not be.' He seems unconvinced by Northumberland's assertion that Bullingbrook has come only to claim what is his by right but, overcome by the strength of Bullingbrook's numbers and the knowledge that his powers are 'weak and all ill-left', he declares himself to be 'as neuter'—then offers hospitality to the enemy of the king!

Bullingbrook, knowing himself victorious (although York continues to vacillate), is obviously expecting to have more power in the future, when he will be able to 'weed and pluck away' the 'caterpillars of the commonwealth', Bushy, Bagot, and Green.

Scene 4   A few lines serve to show the disintegration of Richard's forces. The Welsh Captain's superstitions introduce images of defeat and despair which Salisbury takes up and, in rhyming couplets, puts an end to all Richard's hopes.

Act 3

Scene 1   Bullingbrook establishes his command of the situation by pronouncing death sentences on Bushy and Green, detailing their offences so as to avoid any charge of personal vindictiveness: they have 'misled' the king, caused 'a divorce betwixt his queen and him', been instrumental in Bullingbrook's own banishment and, in his absence, ruined his properties. Most of these accusations were made by Northumberland and others after the death of John of Gaunt (2, 1, 242–62): they form the substance of the anonymous play *Woodstock* (see 'Source, Date, and Text', p. xxxi) and have counterparts in Marlowe's *Edward II*, but the concern of Shakespeare's play is elsewhere.

York, the king's appointed deputy, stands silent whilst the king's favourites are condemned by Bullingbrook and quickly taken to execution by Northumberland. York has evidently surrendered his authority—and, with this, the remnant of the king's forces under his command.

Scene 2   Richard returns from Ireland to claim the audience's attention—but very little besides! We have already witnessed the swelling of Bullingbrook's power, and we must now watch the rapid draining away of Richard's supporters. Sympathies begin to swing away from the wronged Bullingbrook to the defeated Richard, who greets the kingdom on his return from Ireland with an affection that we have not seen before. The imagery of Richard's speeches quickly wins the emotions of the audience, associating Bullingbrook and his confederates with spiders and toads, thieves and robbers, and restoring Richard's glory by comparison with the rising sun. His own rhetoric seems to comfort the king, convincing him—despite the cautions of Carlisle and Aumerle—that he is invincible:

> Not all the water in the rough rude sea
> Can wash the balm off from an anointed king.
> The breath of worldly men cannot depose
> The deputy elected by the Lord.   (lines 54–7)

This philosophy of majesty has dictated Richard's actions for his entire reign—until now!

The dream collapses when Salisbury tells Richard what the audience has known all along, and the rhymes fall with heavy strokes as the king registers his loss and resigns himself to Bullingbrook's success. Scroope brings news of further desertions and Richard is, momentarily, enraged at the suspicion that his favourites have betrayed him. The truth plunges him into despair and he begins to luxuriate in the wretchedness of his position. Pomp and ceremony are only superficial, and the king is no more than other men . . . Carlisle and Aumerle bring him up from the depths of his despair, but once again he is cast down and, certain of his failure, prepares for total surrender.

Even the historian Holinshed had been unable to contain his surprise at the speed of Bullingbrook's bloodless conquest and the way Richard had been 'left desolate, void, and in despair of all hope and comfort'. Any offence in the king, he said, 'ought rather to be imputed to the frailty of wanton youth than to the malice of his heart'. Shakespeare took his cue from Holinshed, deftly manipulating the audience's emotions with skilful rhyming patterns and stylized imagery as he steers the play away from its study of wilful tyranny and into tragedy.

Scene 3 Within this remarkably complex scene, the action moves to different locations—outside the castle, on the battlements of the castle, and again in the lowest court of the castle. Considerable ingenuity in staging is called for, with stylized movements from the actors and ready imagination from the audience!

Bullingbrook is preoccupied with the reports of his intelligence agents, which give him the information that the audience already knows, and seems undisturbed by the little altercation between Northumberland and York. He is surprised to find that Richard has arrived before him at Flint Castle, but sends Northumberland with a message that is both a promise and a threat. He promises 'allegiance and true faith of heart' if his demands for reinstatement are met, but if Richard should refuse this, Bullingbrook will 'use the advantage of [his] power' in a conflict on a massive scale.

Stage directions assist in visualizing the staging: perhaps Northumberland and his trumpeter[s] move upstage to address Richard, whilst York and Bullingbrook observe from a downstage position closer to the audience, drawing their attention to the king's deportment when he appears on the balcony. Richard, as York truly remarks, conducts himself and speaks 'like a king', invoking once more the protection of his divinely ordained majesty to defend him and his country against Bullingbrook and his rebels.

Northumberland assures him that he is mistaken and that Bullingbrook seeks only that which is his by right—but Richard is suspicious. His reply is curt (though Northumberland can use all his 'gracious utterance' to deliver it to Bullingbrook's 'gentle hearing'), but he grants the legitimate request. Despising himself for his condescension, but recognizing again that he is defeated, Richard surrenders his role in a private ceremony with Aumerle that brings first tears then smiles to his kinsman, the pathos toppling over into the absurd. Turning to Northumberland, Richard regains his dignity to hear the command hidden in the next request from 'King Bullingbrook' and then, with bitter self-mockery, begins his descent into 'the base court'.

Bullingbrook still insists that he has 'come but for mine own' but Richard, without further argument, surrenders everything into Bullingbrook's hands. His own despair has defeated him: Bullingbrook used no force except that of personality and popularity, his silent ranks of armed men speaking louder than all language.

Scene 4   After the tensions of high-level politics it is some relief to be in the garden with the queen and her ladies, but even here we are not remote from the issues of the world outside. Gaunt's metaphor of England as a second Eden is developed in the gardener's image of his garden-plot as a kingdom where weeds must be uprooted, too-fast-growing sprays cut down, and caterpillars destroyed. The 'bank of rue', laid as a token of pity for the queen's grief, serves also to commemorate the fall of King Richard.

Act 4

Scene 1   The royal regalia carried at the head of a procession to Parliament establishes the supremacy of Bullingbrook (although he does not ascend the throne until line 113). In a scene which balances the first scene of the play—and which crowds seven different historical events into a single episode—Bullingbrook hears accusations and counter-accusations concerning the death of Gloucester. Now Bagot is the accuser—a Bagot who has apparently switched his loyalties: at 2, 2, 139 he was intending to join Richard in Ireland, but Richard, at *3*, 2, 122, denied all knowledge of his whereabouts. His evidence now is somewhat confusing, for although he may speak the truth about Gloucester's murder, he is obviously mistaken when he refers to Bullingbrook's exile.

Aumerle rejects Bagot's charges with chivalric bravado and gestures that come perilously close to comedy as honours are dared, witnesses invoked, and gages cast down. Bullingbrook adjourns the hearing (just as Richard had suspended the quarrel between himself and Mowbray), then York brings him the news that he has been waiting for—Richard has abdicated, nominating Bullingbrook as his heir and legal successor. Now Bullingbrook ascends the royal throne—but Carlisle can no longer keep silent! He launches an eloquent attack on Bullingbrook and the rebels for their presumption in daring to pass judgement on their monarch, 'the figure of God's majesty'. Passion lends him the gift of prophecy to foresee the chaos of civil war that must ensue if the divine order is violated, confusing 'kin with kin and kind with kind' until 'child, child's children, cry against you woe'. His prophecy recalls that of John of Gaunt (*2*, 1, 31–68) and speaks, for the Elizabethans, in the words articulated in the 'Homily Against Disobedience and Wilful Rebellion', which was read regularly in their churches. England may be suffering with an irresponsible monarch on the throne, but the suffering will be even greater if that throne ever falls to a usurper. Elizabethan sensitivity on this subject was so extreme that the episode which follows Carlisle's admonition, although performed in the public theatres, was not printed in the first three impressions of the play.

Northumberland's immediate reaction to the homily is to arrest the bishop, but Bullingbrook is more responsive. Determined to ensure that the proceedings appear lawful, he commands Richard to the presence so that he can surrender the crown in full view of his people.

The humiliation is agonizing for Richard, conscious of the nobles surrounding him and their well-known faces—'Were they not mine?'. He resigns the crown, literally handing it over to Bullingbrook in a little ceremony that is far more expressive than the mere signing of a document (as in Holinshed's account). Words must be spoken in answer to Bullingbrook's straight question ('Are you contented to resign the crown'), but Richard's agonized indecision can find only punning answers: 'Aye—no. No—aye'. Early texts, printing 'I' for both 'I' and 'aye', could better represent the multiple layers of meaning which include even 'I know no I' as Richard questions his own identity without the royal entitlement.

Bitterly he dramatizes his own deposition, in a reversal of the coronation ceremony. Northumberland is still not satisfied, demanding from Richard a public confession and precipitating an even more acute crisis in Richard's self-awareness. Does he—can he—really exist now that he no longer bears the name of king?

The looking-glass disappoints him, showing his face as before even though it is now 'bankrupt of his majesty'. With a dramatic gesture he smashes it to the ground—but Bullingbrook, increasingly a man of few words, brusquely exposes the futility of such histrionics. Richard soon takes his cue from Bullingbrook's monosyllabic utterances, and the modesty of his final request seems calculated to deflate any magnanimity that Bullingbrook might have intended.

But Bullingbrook's is the ultimate triumph. Granting leave for Richard to go from the scene of his humiliation, he arrests the defeated king and departs to prepare for his own coronation.

Westminster, deputed to be responsible for Carlisle and attended by the sympathetic Aumerle, finds himself among like-minded associates and cheers them with a promise 'to lay A plot shall show us all a merry day'.

Act 5

Scene 1   The queen demands a gesture, however futile—but Richard has progressed beyond this stage. In a short scene that has more literary counterparts than historical ones (see 'Shakespeare's Sources', p. 108), Shakespeare brings the audience to respect the king, majestic now only in his grief and resignation. He has acquired not only self-knowledge but, as the warning to Northumberland shows, a new political awareness. As his captors demonstrate their power by moving him from place to place, Richard performs another ceremony of separation, unkissing the wedding vow that had joined him with the queen. They are briefly linked by the rhymes of the couplets, but even here (line 84) they cannot avoid the intrusion of Northumberland.

Scene 2   The Duke of York finds his loyalties severely tested! According to the duchess, he was 'weeping' as he told her about Bullingbrook's grand entry into the city of London with its welcoming citizens and now, describing the reception given to Richard, it is evident where his sympathies lie. To York, Richard is still the anointed king, and his dejected head is 'sacred'. But things have changed—and the rhymed couplet of lines 37–8 seems to pronounce York's acquiescence in 'these events' ordained by the 'high will' of heaven. He is now subject to Bullingbrook, the 'new-made king', and has also given his pledge for the loyalty of his son, now merely Earl of Rutland and no longer Duke of Aumerle, the title bestowed on him by King Richard.

But his son is of a different mind, and the resulting conflict shows parental ties stretched to their limits for father and mother alike.

Scene 3   The unexpected reference to Bullingbrook's 'unthrifty son' suggests that Shakespeare is already thinking about the sequel to *Richard II*; in *Henry IV Part 1* the estrangement between Bullingbrook and his son, the future Henry V, is central to the action, and his tavern life with his 'unrestrained loose companions' is the play's main focus.

When the entire York family breaks into Bullingbrook's reverie the scene hovers on the edges of comedy. Language and gestures, promised and actual, are all extreme, and rhymes emphasize their absurdity—which Bullingbrook himself, joining in, is quick to appreciate.

But when family honours are appeased, the rhyming stops. Bullingbrook has learned of the conspiracy and will take immediate action against the ringleaders. Now he must understand that Richard, so long as he is alive, remains a threat.

Scene 4   Bullingbrook has spoken: Exton tells us all that we need to know as we approach Richard in his prison.

Scene 5   This long soliloquy has no parallel in Shakespeare's sources. Richard, with ironic detachment, speaks to an imaginary listener (who is addressed directly at line 55) and describes the thoughts going through his head in his solitary confinement. Seeking for spiritual consolation produces biblical quotations that contradict each other; optimistic dreams result in wild ideas about escaping; and he can console himself only by calling to mind some earlier precedents for his misery. With wry humour he indulges himself in the same kind of word-play that occupied the queen's depression in *Act 2*, Scene 2, its sophistication increasing with his desperation.

The welcome music—welcome to the actor as well as to the character—prompts a fresh metaphor, and 'time' in harmony leads to the elaborate conceit of the striking clock.

The interruption of the friendly groom recalls Richard to the immediate present, and the detail of his favourite horse provokes a momentary burst of anger which is as soon withdrawn as it is spoken. Richard has learned his lesson in patience and long-suffering—but the intrusion of Exton sounds a warning signal.

Richard, never before associated with physical action, finds amazing strength for the final confrontation with the men sent to murder him. Holinshed says that Exton was accompanied by eight servants, and that Richard killed four of these, but the text, no doubt accommodating itself to the demands of the theatrical company, seems to allow for only two deaths. Nonetheless, Richard's courage is enough to convince Exton that he has done wrong, that 'this deed is chronicled in hell'.

Scene 6   Bullingbrook is victorious: one after another his enemies surrender or are defeated. The last news is the best—or is it? Exton brings in the coffin:

> Herein all breathless lies
> The mightiest of thy greatest enemies,
> Richard of Bordeaux.

The play ends as it had begun—with a guilty monarch and the reminder of a biblical precedent in Cain's murder of his brother and the blood of Abel crying to heaven for vengeance (see *1*, 1, 104, and Genesis 4:12, 14). Throughout his reign Bullingbrook—Henry IV—will be tormented by the recollection of his crime, and his son, Henry V, will never make more than partial and temporary expiation.

Authentic?

History is always *untidy*. Endlessly fascinating—and never completely satisfying. The affairs of human beings defy any simple interpretation, and facts very often obscure the real issues. False trails and loose ends may tempt the scholar into a wilderness of speculation—but to the creative artist they can be the essential clues to lead him to the heart of the matter. A character in Ben Jonson's play *The Devil is an Ass*, commended for his 'cunning i'th' *Chronicle*', modestly disclaims academic study and explains,

> No, I confess I ha't from the Play-books,
> And think they are more authentic. (II. iv. 13–14)

This theatre-buff might well be speaking of any history play written by William Shakespeare, and of *Richard II* in particular. Here Shakespeare perverts certain facts and scrambles certain dates but achieves an emotional authenticity far beyond the reach of the most detailed and accurate of his sources.

It would be pedantic and superfluous to enumerate all of Shakespeare's 'adjustments' to the materials provided by history, but a few are worth remarking for the light they shed on the art of the dramatist. The Duke of Gloucester, a man of intrigue and violence, was suffocated, not beheaded—but Shakespeare needs the blood of a martyr for his imagery. The Duchess of Gloucester died some years later than the play suggests, but the announcement of her death in *Act 2*, Scene 2 adds to the relentless 'tide of woes' flooding over the kingdom. The queen of the play is a mature woman and loving wife, not the 10-year-old girl who was married to Richard at the end of his reign; and the impetuous Henry Percy of *Act 2*, Scene 3 was in real life a man two years *older* than Bullingbrook.

The queen's love for her husband is an ingenious instrument, a kind of lever, which Shakespeare uses to swing the sympathies of the audience from one extreme to another as the fortunes of the king change him from ruthless autocrat to tragic hero. The historical Richard was a complex and complicated character, totally incapable of wielding the enormous power with which he was invested and in which he took such great delight. Shakespeare's presentation of him has won high praise from a modern biographer/historian: 'All the most vital aspects of Richard's being—his intense self-regard, his craving for attention, his taste for the theatrical, his appetite for grandeur and at the same time his greatest weakness, his inner emptiness—find a place in his reading'. Although the insights offered by Shakespeare were those of a dramatist and not a historian, 'his characterization of the king and his understanding of what mattered to him probably bring us closer to the historical figure than many a work of history'.[1]

But *Richard II* is more than the history of Richard II. With this play Shakespeare begins a new 'tetralogy'—a series of four plays, each one entire in itself, linked together by a common theme or subject. Shakespeare's first tetralogy of English history plays consisted of the three parts of *Henry VI* and *Richard III*, and the grand overall design of these eight plays allows him fully to explore the far-reaching effects of a single deed—the deposing of an anointed king.

Richard II is followed by the two parts of *Henry IV*, showing how Bullingbrook's reign was always troubled by the threats of civil war prophesied in *Richard II* by the Bishop of Carlisle (*4*, 1, 136) and provoked by the insurrection of his former allies, the Earl of Northumberland and his son Henry Percy. In *Henry IV Part 1* Percy, nicknamed Hotspur, is contrasted with Prince Hal, Bullingbrook's 'unthrifty son' (*Richard II*, *5*, 3, 1), who must redeem himself through the struggle with Hotspur if he is to prove worthy to wear the crown that descends to him—with its burden of guilt—from his father. Henry V was, for the Elizabethans, a national hero. Alert to the dangers of civil war, he had directed energies outwards, fighting and—although heavily outnumbered—conquering magnificently in France. But a sense of sin is ever present with Shakespeare's king, who prays before the battle of Agincourt

> Not today, O Lord,
> Oh, not today, think not upon the fault
> My father made in compassing the crown.
>
> (*Henry V*, *4*, 1, 291–3)

Retribution, however, was not immediately forthcoming, and the second tetralogy ends with the triumph of *Henry V*.

[1] *Richard II*, by Nigel Saul, (Yale University Press, New Haven and London, 1997), pp. 466–7.

Bullingbrook's 'fault' remained for expiation after the death of his son in 1422—as Shakespeare had shown in the plays of his first tetralogy, written between 1590 and 1593. Here the worst face of civil war is shown, emblematically, in a stage direction from the Folio text of *Henry VI Part 3*, '*Enter a son that hath killed his father, and a father that hath killed his son*' (2, 5, 55s.d.). Henry VI was eventually succeeded by Richard III whose reign, as presented in Shakespeare's play, was a grotesque nightmare. Not until the accession of Henry Tudor in 1485 did the country again enjoy that order and harmony which—so pious patriots believed—was ordained by God for 'this sceptred isle'.

Shakespeare's Verse

Easily the best way to understand and appreciate Shakespeare's verse is to read it aloud! Don't be captivated by the dominant rhythm, but decide which are the most important words in each line and use the regular metre to drive them forward to the listeners.

Shakespeare's plays are written mainly in blank verse, the form preferred by most dramatists in the sixteenth and early seventeenth centuries. It is a very flexible medium, capable—like the human speaking voice—of a wide range of tones. Basically the lines, which are unrhymed, are ten syllables long. The syllables have alternating stresses, just like normal English speech, and they divide into five 'feet'. The technical name for this is 'iambic pentameter'. The formal language of the first scene establishes this rhythm for *Richard II*:

> Old Jóhn of Gáunt, time-hónour'd Láncastér,
> Hast thóu accórding tó thy óath and bánd
> Brought híther Hénry Hérford, thý bold són,
> Here tó make góod the bóisterous láte appéal,
> Which thén our léisure wóuld not lét us héar,
> Agáinst the Dúke of Nórfolk, Thómas Mówbray?   (*1*, 1, 1–6)

Unusually for Shakespeare, this play is written entirely in verse, and it has a surprisingly large proportion of rhyming lines, mostly in couplets but sometimes forming more elaborate patterns (for example in the lament of the Duchess of Gloucester, *1*, 2, 60–74).

A line—and a rhyme—can be shared between two speakers without losing either the rhythm or the sense:

> **Gaunt**
> To bé a máke-peace sháll becóme my áge.
> Throw dówn, my són, the Dúke of Nórfolk's gáge.
> **Richard**
> And, Nórfolk, thrów down hís.   .
> **Gaunt**
>   When, Hárry, whén?
> Obédience bíds I shóuld not bíd agáin.

Richard
Norfólk, throw dówn we̞ bíd; there ís no bóot.
Mowbray
Mysélf I thrów, dread sóvereign, át thy fóot.   (*1*, *1*, 160–5)

Such shared lines—and rhymes—can make for rapid delivery when the speakers are of the same mind, or else engaged in quick-fire repartee, but here a long, suspenseful pause might follow Richard's injunction to Mowbray before Gaunt's impatience completes the line.

At this early stage in Shakespeare's writing career, the verse lines are mainly end-stopped, with a marked mid-line break (a 'caesura'). The colloquial abbreviations and elisions (i'th', o'th') used in everyday conversation are occasionally found, but the dignity of the persons, the formality of the scenes, and the magnitude of the action all demand correspondingly exalted styles. Shakespeare has found the appropriate medium for *Richard II* in this regular verse form, enriched by biblical allusions and enlivened by the bursts of rhyming which, apparently awkward on the page, can be barely noticeable in performance.

Source, Date, and Text

The many sources, influences, and analogies that have been found for this play can only testify to Shakespeare's fascination with the character and reign of Richard II. His main source was Raphael Holinshed's *Chronicles of England, Scotland, and Ireland* (2nd edition, 1574), and several other historians, both English and French, provided minor details. Inspiration of a different kind came from creative writers such as Samuel Daniel with his long narrative poem of *The Civil Wars Between The Two Houses Of Lancaster and York* (1595), Christopher Marlowe and his play *Edward II* (1592), and the anonymous author of the play *Woodstock* (1592 or 1593).

Richard II was probably performed on stage by the end of 1595. Although there is no precise evidence for this, it may be deduced from a letter written on 7 December 1595 by Sir Edward Hoby to Sir Robert Cecil—an invitation to his home 'where as late as it shall please you a gate for your supper shall be open & K. Richard present'. Most probably Sir Edward had commissioned a special performance by Shakespeare's company of one of their newest plays.

The play was released to the printers in 1597, presumably because its initial stage popularity was declining. On the bookstalls, however, it enjoyed more success: with two reprints in 1598 it became the first play-text to warrant three printings in the space of two years. The second of these bore Shakespeare's name on its title-page—the first time he had ever been acknowledged in print as the author of one of his plays.

Because it was printed with the full knowledge and permission of the dramatic company, the text of *Richard II* is unusually free from errors in the early quartos, although the 'deposition scene' (4, 1, 155–319) was omitted from the first three of these (see 'Crisis in the Monarchy', p. iv). The text of the First Folio edition (1623), based on a copy of the third quarto supplemented by a playhouse manuscript, is mainly useful for its stage directions and as an indication of theatre practices. The present edition is founded on Andrew Gurr's text of 1984 for the New Cambridge Shakespeare Series.

Characters in the Play

King Richard the Second

The King's Uncles	John of Gaunt, Duke of Lancaster Edmund of Langley, Duke of York
The King's Cousins	Henry Bullingbrook, Duke of Hereford, *son of the* Duke of Lancaster; *afterwards* King Henry IV Duke of Aumerle, Earl of Rutland, *son to the* Duke of York
Supporters of the King	Thomas Mowbray, Duke of Norfolk Sir John Bushy, *Speaker of the House of Commons* Sir William Bagot, *minister and councillor* Sir Henry Green, *councillor* Bishop of Carlisle Abbot of Westminster
Followers of Bullingbrook	Earl of Northumberland Harry Percy, *son to the* Earl of Northumberland Lord Ross Lord Willoughby Sir Piers of Exton

Act I

Act I   Scene I

King Richard gives formal hearing to the
quarrel between Bullingbrook and Mowbray.
Bullingbrook accuses Mowbray of high
treason and conspiracy in the murder of
Gloucester. Mowbray denies both charges.
The king attempts to reconcile the
adversaries, but they insist on trial by
combat. A date is appointed for the contest.

1 *Old John of Gaunt*: Richard's uncle was
   58 when the events of the play took
   place (1397–1400).
2 *band*: bond (an archaic form).
3 *Herford*: Hereford; the shorter form
   indicates the probable pronunciation.
4 *late*: recent.
   appeal: accusation.
5 *our leisure . . . hear*: I was not at leisure
   to hear you; Richard uses the 'royal
   plural', emphasizing the formality of the
   occasion.
7 *liege*: liege-lord; Gaunt asserts his own
   loyalty to the king.
8 *sounded*: enquired of.
9 *on ancient malice*: on grounds of some
   long-standing and personal quarrel.
11 *some known ground*: basis of something
   he has learned.
12 *As near . . . argument*: from what I could
   find out by questioning him on the
   subject.
13 *some apparent danger*: an obvious threat.
15 *our presence*: a formal hearing before us.
17 *accused*: accusèd.
18 *High stomach'd*: self-opinionated, proud.

21 *most loving liege*: The feudal monarch—
   ideally—loved his subjects and they, in
   return, gave him complete loyalty.

Scene 1

Windsor Castle. Enter King Richard, John
of Gaunt, *with other* Nobles *and*
Attendants

Richard
Old John of Gaunt, time-honour'd Lancaster,
Hast thou according to thy oath and band
Brought hither Henry Herford, thy bold son,
Here to make good the boisterous late appeal,
5 Which then our leisure would not let us hear,
Against the Duke of Norfolk, Thomas Mowbray?
Gaunt
I have, my liege.
Richard
Tell me moreover hast thou sounded him
If he appeal the Duke on ancient malice,
10 Or worthily as a good subject should
On some known ground of treachery in him?
Gaunt
As near as I could sift him on that argument,
On some apparent danger seen in him
Aim'd at your highness, no inveterate malice.
Richard
15 Then call them to our presence. Face to face
And frowning brow to brow ourselves will hear
The accuser and the accused freely speak.
High stomach'd are they both and full of ire,
In rage deaf as the sea, hasty as fire.

Enter Bullingbrook *and* Mowbray

Bullingbrook
20 Many years of happy days befall
My gracious sovereign, my most loving liege.

22 *Each day . . . happiness*: may every day be happier than the last one.	
23 *envying . . . hap*: envious of the good fortune of earth; 'envying' is stressed on the second syllable.	
24 *Add . . . crown*: immortàlize you, enthrone you in heaven.	
26 *cause you come*: cause that brings you here.	
27 *appeal*: accuse.	
28 *object*: bring as an accusation.	

Mowbray

Each day still better other's happiness,
Until the heavens, envying earth's good hap,
Add an immortal title to your crown.

Richard

25 We thank you both. Yet one but flatters us,
As well appeareth by the cause you come,
Namely to appeal each other of high treason.
Cousin of Herford, what dost thou object
Against the Duke of Norfolk, Thomas Mowbray?

Bullingbrook

30 First, heaven be the record to my speech.
In the devotion of a subject's love,
Tendering the precious safety of my prince,
And free from other misbegotten hate,
Come I appellant to this princely presence.
35 Now Thomas Mowbray do I turn to thee,
And mark my greeting well; for what I speak
My body shall make good upon this earth,
Or my divine soul answer it in heaven.
Thou art a traitor and a miscreant,
40 Too good to be so, and too bad to live.
Since the more fair and crystal is the sky,
The uglier seem the clouds that in it fly.
Once more, the more to aggravate the note,
With a foul traitor's name stuff I thy throat,
45 And wish (so please my sovereign) ere I move,
What my tongue speaks my right drawn sword may
    prove.

Mowbray

Let not my cold words here accuse my zeal.
'Tis not the trial of a woman's war,
The bitter clamour of two eager tongues,
50 Can arbitrate this cause betwixt us twain.
The blood is hot that must be cool'd for this.
Yet can I not of such tame patience boast
As to be hush'd, and naught at all to say.
First, the fair reverence of your highness curbs me
55 From giving reins and spurs to my free speech,
Which else would post until it had return'd
These terms of treason doubled down his throat.
Setting aside his high blood's royalty,
And let him be no kinsman to my liege,

30 *record*: witness.

32 *Tendering*: cherishing and protecting.

34 *appellant*: in formal accusation.

36 *my greeting*: the way I shall address you.

37 *make good*: justify.

38 *divine*: immortal.

40 *good*: nobly born.

41 *crystal*: clear, bright.

43 *aggravate*: emphasize.
   note: mark of public disgrace (from Latin *nota*, the Roman Censor's official reproof).

46 *right drawn*: justly drawn.

47 *accuse*: cast any doubt on.

48 *trial*: disputation.
   woman's war: i.e. verbal conflict, shouting match.

49 *eager*: sharp-edged.

51 *cool'd*: i.e. by spilling; medicinal bloodletting was routine treatment for some fevers.

54 *fair reverence of*: proper respect for.

56 *post*: gallop ahead.

57 *terms*: insults.
   doubled: redoubled.

58–9 *Setting aside . . . liege*: disregarding his royal birth and his relationship to your majesty; Bullingbrook was first cousin to Richard.

62 *allow him odds*: give him an advantage.
63 *tied*: obliged.

65 *inhabitable*: uninhabitable.

67 *this*: i.e. his protestation of innocence.
68 *hopes*: i.e. hopes of salvation.

69 *gage*: pledge, usually a glove, thrown
   down as a token.

70–1 *Disclaiming . . . royalty*: Bullingbrook
   absolves Mowbray from any charge of
   shedding royal blood.
72 *except*: hold back.
74 *stoop*: i.e. to pick up the gage.
77 *or . . . devise*: or any even worse lies that
   you can invent.
78–9 *that sword . . . shoulder*: i.e. the king's
   sword, conferring knighthood with a tap
   on the shoulder.
80–1 *any fair degree . . . trial*: any fair
   measure or form of combat allowed by
   the laws of chivalry.
82 *light*: alight, dismount.
83 *unjustly*: in an unjust cause.
85 *inherit*: bequeath, pass on to.

87 *Look what*: whatever.
88 *nobles*: gold coins, worth one-third of a
   pound.
89 *lendings*: advances on pay; Holinshed
   says Mowbray should have used this
   money to pay the garrison at Calais.
90 *lewd*: improper.
95 *these eighteen years*: i.e. since the
   Peasants' Revolt of 1381; see 'Crisis in
   the Monarchy', p. iv.
96 *Complotted*: plotted in combination with
   others.
   contrived: contrivèd; devised, brought
   about.
97 *Fetch*: derive.

60 I do defy him, and I spit at him,
   Call him a slanderous coward and a villain,
   Which to maintain I would allow him odds
   And meet him were I tied to run afoot
   Even to the frozen ridges of the Alps,
65 Or any other ground inhabitable
   Where ever Englishman durst set his foot.
   Meantime, let this defend my loyalty:
   By all my hopes most falsely doth he lie.
     Bullingbrook
   Pale trembling coward, there I throw my gage,
70 Disclaiming here the kindred of the king,
   And lay aside my high blood's royalty,
   Which fear, not reverence, makes thee to except.
   If guilty dread have left thee so much strength
   As to take up mine honour's pawn, then stoop.
75 By that and all the rites of knighthood else
   Will I make good against thee, arm to arm,
   What I have spoke, or thou canst worse devise.
     Mowbray
   I take it up, and by that sword I swear
   Which gently laid my knighthood on my shoulder
80 I'll answer thee in any fair degree
   Or chivalrous design of knightly trial;
   And when I mount, alive may I not light
   If I be traitor or unjustly fight.
     Richard
   What doth our cousin lay to Mowbray's charge?
85 It must be great that can inherit us
   So much as of a thought of ill in him.
     Bullingbrook
   Look what I speak, my life shall prove it true:
   That Mowbray hath receiv'd eight thousand nobles
   In name of lendings for your highness' soldiers,
90 The which he hath detain'd for lewd employments
   Like a false traitor and injurious villain.
   Besides I say, and will in battle prove
   Or here or elsewhere to the furthest verge
   That ever was surveyed by English eye,
95 That all the treasons for these eighteen years
   Complotted and contrived in this land
   Fetch from false Mowbray their first head and
     spring.

98–9 *Further I say . . . good*: In addition I
    say, and I will undertake to prove it on
    his rotten life. Bullingbrook tries to
    balance 'good' ('make . . . good' =
    prove) against 'bad'.

100 *Gloucester's death*: Gloucester was
    murdered when he was in the custody
    of Mowbray; see 'Commentary', p. xiii.

101 *Suggest*: incite, prompt.

102 *consequently*: subsequently.

103 *streams of blood*: This suggests that
    Gloucester was beheaded, and allows
    Shakespeare to proceed to the
    comparison with Abel; most of
    Shakespeare's sources, however, say that
    Gloucester was smothered.

104 *sacrificing Abel*: Abel, whose sacrifice of
    sheep found favour with God, was
    murdered by his jealous brother Cain
    (Genesis 4:10).

104–5 *cries . . . earth*: 'the voice of thy
    brother's blood crieth unto me from the
    ground' (Genesis 4:12).

106 *To me*: Bullingbrook was Gloucester's
    nephew—and so was Richard: see
    'Family Tree', p. vi–vii.

109 *pitch*: the highest point in the flight of a
    falcon before swooping down on the
    prey.

Further I say, and further will maintain
Upon his bad life to make all this good,
100 That he did plot the Duke of Gloucester's death,
Suggest his soon-believing adversaries,
And consequently like a traitor coward
Sluic'd out his innocent soul through streams of
    blood,
Which blood, like sacrificing Abel's, cries
105 Even from the tongueless caverns of the earth
To me for justice and rough chastisement;
And, by the glorious worth of my descent,
This arm shall do it, or this life be spent.
    Richard
How high a pitch his resolution soars!
110 Thomas of Norfolk, what say'st thou to this?

113 *slander of his blood*: disgrace to his royal
    blood.

115 *eyes and ears*: Richard responds to
    Mowbray's 'face' and 'ears' in the
    previous lines.

116 *my kingdom's heir*: In fact Bullingbrook
    was a possible heir to the throne, but
    Richard had nominated the son of
    Roger Mortimer as his successor; see
    'Family Tree', p. vi–vii.

117 *my father . . . son*: i.e. Richard's cousin;
    Richard states the relationship in the
    most distant terms.

118 *my sceptre's awe*: the reverence due to
    my sceptre (i.e. majesty).

119 *sacred blood*: Richard insists on the
    divine nature of kingship.

    Mowbray
Oh let my sovereign turn away his face
And bid his ears a little while be deaf,
Till I have told this slander of his blood
How God and good men hate so foul a liar.
    Richard
115 Mowbray, impartial are our eyes and ears.
Were he my brother, nay, my kingdom's heir,
As he is but my father's brother's son,
Now by my sceptre's awe I make a vow
Such neighbour nearness to our sacred blood

124 *as low as to thy heart*: The usual
  expression was 'to lie in the throat' (see
  line 44).
126 *receipt*: sum received.
  Calais: The spelling of the early
  editions—'Callice'—indicates
  Elizabethan pronunciation.
128 *by consent*: by agreement (with the king).
129 *For that*: because.
130 *remainder*: balance.
  dear: expensive *and* loving; heavy
  expenses were incurred in Mowbray's
  expedition to France to negotiate
  Richard's marriage.
132 *For*: as for.
133–4 *I slew him . . . that case*: Mowbray is
  evasive: in fact he had delayed for three
  weeks before carrying out the order to
  kill Gloucester.
137–41 *Once . . . had it*: Holinshed refers to
  such an incident, but gives no
  particulars.
138 *grieved*: grievèd.
139 *the sacrament*: i.e. the sacrament of Holy
  Communion, the central rite of the
  Christian religion.
140 *confess it*: Confession of sins is essential
  before receiving Holy Communion.
  exactly: specifically, for that particular
  deed.
142 *the rest appeal'd*: the other allegations.
144 *A recreant . . . traitor*: a coward false to
  his own royal blood.
146 *interchangeably*: reciprocally.
  hurl: will hurl.
149 *the best . . . bosom*: i.e. his life's blood.
150 *In haste whereof*: to hasten which.

120 Should nothing privilege him nor partialize
   The unstooping firmness of my upright soul.
   He is our subject, Mowbray; so art thou.
   Free speech and fearless I to thee allow.
     Mowbray
   Then, Bullingbrook, as low as to thy heart
125 Through the false passage of thy throat thou liest.
   Three parts of that receipt I had for Calais
   Disburs'd I duly to his highness' soldiers.
   The other part reserv'd I by consent,
   For that my sovereign liege was in my debt
130 Upon remainder of a dear account
   Since last I went to France to fetch his queen.
   Now swallow down that lie. For Gloucester's death,
   I slew him not, but to my own disgrace
   Neglected my sworn duty in that case.
135 For you, my noble lord of Lancaster,
   The honourable father to my foe,
   Once did I lay an ambush for your life,
   A trespass that doth vex my grieved soul.
   But ere I last receiv'd the sacrament
140 I did confess it, and exactly begg'd
   Your grace's pardon, and I hope I had it.
   This is my fault. As for the rest appeal'd,
   It issues from the rancour of a villain,
   A recreant and most degenerate traitor,
145 Which in myself I boldly will defend,
   And interchangeably hurl down my gage
   Upon this overweening traitor's foot,
   To prove myself a loyal gentleman
   Even in the best blood chamber'd in his bosom.
150 In haste whereof most heartily I pray
   Your highness to assign our trial day.
     Richard
   Wrath-kindl'd gentlemen, be rul'd by me.
   Let's purge this choler without letting blood.

153 *purge . . . blood*: pacify this fury without
  shedding any blood; the usual medical
  treatment for 'choler' (which was
  thought to be caused by excess of
  yellow bile) was by letting blood drain
  from the body through shallow cuts in
  the veins.

154 *though no physician*: although I am not a
physician; it was traditional, however, to
speak of the king as physician of his
country.

156 *conclude*: come to terms.

157 *Our doctors . . . bleed*: Some seasons
were supposed to be more favourable
than others for the practice of bloodletting.

163 *Obedience*: filial duty.

164 *boot*: point, alternative.

165 *Myself I throw*: Mowbray probably
kneels before the king.

167 *The one my duty owes*: as a subject I owe
you my life (i.e. the service of my life).

167–8 *name/Despite . . . grave*: name that will
live on my tomb even when I am dead.

170 *impeach'd*: accused in law.
baffled: publicly dishonoured; in
ceremonies of chivalry this would
involve hanging the knight (or his
effigy) upside down by the heels.

174 *Lions . . . tame*: The lion, king of beasts,
is featured on the royal coat of arms,
leopards on the Norfolk arms carried by
Mowbray.

175 *change his spots*: 'Can the Ethiopian
change his skin, or the leopard his
spots' (Jeremiah 13:23); Mowbray puns
on 'spots' = stains.
Take but: only take away.

184 *try*: defend.

This we prescribe though no physician.
155 Deep malice makes too deep incision.
Forget, forgive, conclude and be agreed.
Our doctors say this is no month to bleed.
Good uncle, let this end where it begun,
We'll calm the Duke of Norfolk, you your son.

Gaunt
160 To be a make-peace shall become my age.
Throw down, my son, the Duke of Norfolk's gage.

Richard
And, Norfolk, throw down his.

Gaunt
                              When, Harry, when?
Obedience bids I should not bid again.

Richard
Norfolk, throw down we bid; there is no boot.

Mowbray
165 Myself I throw, dread sovereign, at thy foot.
My life thou shalt command, but not my shame.
The one my duty owes, but my fair name,
Despite of death, that lives upon my grave,
To dark dishonour's use thou shalt not have.
170 I am disgrac'd, impeach'd and baffled here,
Pierc'd to the soul with slander's venom'd spear,
The which no balm can cure but his heart blood
Which breath'd this poison.

Richard
                              Rage must be withstood.
Give me his gage. Lions make leopards tame.

Mowbray
175 Yea, but not change his spots. Take but my shame
And I resign my gage. My dear, dear lord,
The purest treasure mortal times afford
Is spotless reputation; that away,
Men are but gilded loam, or painted clay.
180 A jewel in a ten times barr'd up chest
Is a bold spirit in a loyal breast.
Mine honour is my life, both grow in one.
Take honour from me and my life is done.
Then, dear my liege, mine honour let me try.
185 In that I live, and for that will I die.

186 *Cousin*: Richard reaffirms the blood
relationship as he turns to Bullingbrook.
throw up: yield, surrender.

188 *crestfallen*: humbled.
189 *impeach*: disgrace.
height: high rank.
190 *out-dar'd dastard*: coward overcome by
daring.
192 *sound . . . parle*: call a truce on such
base grounds; the metaphor is of
sounding a trumpet.
192–4 *my teeth . . . bleeding*: Such an action
was performed on stage by a character
in Thomas Kyd's play *The Spanish
Tragedy* (c. 1577), and suggested by
Titus in Shakespeare's own *Titus
Andronicus* (*3*, *1*, 131–2).
193 *motive*: moving limb, i.e. his tongue.
194 *his*: its.
195 *Exit Gaunt*: Elizabethan stage
convention demanded that there should
be at least ten lines between the
departure of a character and his return
to the stage.
199 *Saint Lambert's Day*: 17 September (the
date given by Holinshed: other
historians differ); Lambert was a bishop
of Maastricht in the first century.
202 *atone you*: make you as one, reconcile
you.
203 *Justice*: i.e. the justice of God;
righteousness (according to chivalric
theory) would be certain to triumph in
such a combat.
205 *home alarms*: calls to arms at home (as
opposed to the calls to fight in Ireland).

Richard
Cousin, throw up your gage. Do you begin.
Bullingbrook
O God defend my soul from such deep sin!
Shall I seem crestfallen in my father's sight?
Or with pale beggar fear impeach my height
190 Before this out-dar'd dastard? Ere my tongue
Shall wound my honour with such feeble wrong,
Or sound so base a parle, my teeth shall tear
The slavish motive of recanting fear
And spit it bleeding in his high disgrace,
195 Where shame doth harbour, even in Mowbray's face.
                                    [*Exit* Gaunt

Richard
We were not born to sue, but to command,
Which, since we cannot do to make you friends,
Be ready, as your lives shall answer it,
At Coventry upon Saint Lambert's Day.
200 There shall your swords and lances arbitrate
The swelling difference of your settled hate.
Since we cannot atone you, we shall see
Justice design the victor's chivalry.
Lord Marshal, command our officers at arms
205 Be ready to direct these home alarms.
                                    [*Exeunt*

Act 1   Scene 2

The Duchess of Gloucester pleads with John
of Gaunt to avenge the murder of her
husband but Gaunt, although he knows the
culprit, cannot be disloyal to the king.

1 *part . . . blood*: my relationship with
Woodstock (the murdered Duke of
Gloucester, Gaunt's brother).

4 *those hands*: i.e. the king's hands.

6 *Put we*: let us commit.

Scene 2

John of Gaunt's *house. Enter* John of
Gaunt *with the* Duchess of Gloucester

Gaunt
Alas, the part I had in Woodstock's blood
Doth more solicit me than your exclaims
To stir against the butchers of his life.
But since correction lieth in those hands
5 Which made the fault that we cannot correct,
Put we our quarrel to the will of heaven,

7 *they*: Gaunt's singular 'heaven' (= God) has slid into a plural form (= the skies).

11–21 *Edward's seven sons . . . axe*: Throughout this speech Shakespeare preserves the double metaphor (which derives from a medieval genealogical emblem) of vials containing blood drawn from a single source, and branches springing from a single root.

15 *the Destinies*: the three Fates (in classical mythology) who spun, wove, and cut the thread of human life.

21 *envy*: malice, hatred.

23 *self*: same.
   mettle: stuff, substance.

25 *consent*: acquiesce, agree.

28 *model*: perfect copy.
29 *patience*: forbearance, Christian long-suffering.
   despair: desperation (which was a sinful as well as pitiable state of mind).
31 *naked*: undefended.
33 *mean*: ordinary, common.

36 *venge*: avenge.

3. *anointed . . . sight*: i.e. in the coronation ceremony.

43 *God . . . defence*: 'A father of the fatherless, and a judge of the widows, is God in his holy habitation' (Psalm 68:5).

Who when they see the hours ripe on earth
Will rain hot vengeance on offenders' heads.
   Duchess
Finds brotherhood in thee no sharper spur?
10 Hath love in thy old blood no living fire?
Edward's seven sons, whereof thyself art one,
Were as seven vials of his sacred blood,
Or seven fair branches springing from one root.
Some of those seven are dried by nature's course,
15 Some of those branches by the Destinies cut,
But Thomas, my dear lord, my life, my Gloucester,
One vial full of Edward's sacred blood,
One flourishing branch of his most royal root,
Is crack'd, and all the precious liquor spilt,
20 Is hack'd down, and his summer leaves all faded,
By envy's hand, and murder's bloody axe.
Ah, Gaunt, his blood was thine; that bed, that womb,
That mettle, that self mould, that fashion'd thee
Made him a man; and though thou liv'st and breath'st
25 Yet art thou slain in him. Thou dost consent
In some large measure to thy father's death
In that thou seest thy wretched brother die,
Who was the model of thy father's life.
Call it not patience, Gaunt. It is despair.
30 In suffering thus thy brother to be slaughter'd
Thou showest the naked pathway to thy life,
Teaching stern murder how to butcher thee.
That which in mean men we entitle patience
Is pale cold cowardice in noble breasts.
35 What shall I say? To safeguard thine own life
The best way is to venge my Gloucester's death.
   Gaunt
God's is the quarrel, for God's substitute,
His deputy anointed in His sight,
Hath caus'd his death, the which if wrongfully
40 Let heaven revenge, for I may never lift
An angry arm against His minister.
   Duchess
Where then, alas, may I complain myself?
   Gaunt
To God, the widow's champion and defence.

Duchess

Why then I will. Farewell, old Gaunt.

45 Thou goest to Coventry, there to behold

Our cousin Herford and fell Mowbray fight.

Oh, set my husband's wrongs on Herford's spear,

That it may enter butcher Mowbray's breast!

Or if misfortune miss the first career

50 Be Mowbray's sins so heavy in his bosom

That they may break his foaming courser's back,

And throw the rider headlong in the lists,

A caitiff recreant to my cousin Herford.

Farewell, old Gaunt. Thy sometime brother's wife

55 With her companion grief must end her life.

Gaunt

Sister, farewell. I must to Coventry.

As much good stay with thee as go with me.

Duchess

Yet one word more. Grief boundeth where it falls,

Not with the empty hollowness, but weight.

60 I take my leave before I have begun,

For sorrow ends not when it seemeth done.

Commend me to thy brother Edmund York.

Lo, this is all. Nay, yet depart not so;

Though this be all, do not so quickly go.

65 I shall remember more. Bid him, ah, what?

With all good speed at Plashy visit me.

Alack, and what shall good old York there see

But empty lodgings and unfurnish'd walls,

Unpeopled offices, untrodden stones,

70 And what hear there for welcome but my groans?

Therefore commend me, let him not come there,

To seek out sorrow that dwells everywhere.

Desolate, desolate will I hence and die.

The last leave of thee takes my weeping eye.

[*Exeunt*

46 *cousin*: kinsman, relative; Hereford (Bullingbrook) was the Duchess's nephew.
fell: cruel.

49 *career*: charge, encounter in the tilt ('career' = a gallop ending in a sudden stop).

52 *lists*: barriers of the fenced jousting area.

53 *caitiff recreant*: captive coward.

54 *sometime*: former.

58 *boundeth*: rebounds (like a ball).

66 *Plashy*: The Essex home of the Gloucester family.

68 *lodgings*: rooms.
unfurnish'd walls: walls bare of tapestries or arms.

69 *Unpeopled offices*: no servants to perform their duties.

Act 1   Scene 3

When all the formalities have been observed,
Bullingbrook and Mowbray prepare to fight
to the death—but suddenly the king
intervenes. After some discussion with his
Council, Richard pronounces sentence on
the two contestants.

2 *at all points*: completely (i.e. he is
   wearing all the pieces of his suit of
   armour).
   enter in: enter the lists for the combat.
3 *sprightfully*: full of high spirits.
4 *Stays but*: is only waiting for.
   appellant: accuser.

6s.d. *set*: seated; on such an occasion the
   nobles, as well as the king, might sit
   down to watch the show.
   Duke of Norfolk . . . defendant: Properly
   speaking, the defendant should not
   enter until he is summoned, and not
   speak until he is charged.
7 *demand of*: Richard uses the words of
   formal enquiry.

Scene 3

Coventry. Enter Lord Marshal *and the*
Duke Aumerle

Marshal
My Lord Aumerle, is Harry Herford arm'd?
   Aumerle
Yea, at all points, and longs to enter in.
   Marshal
The Duke of Norfolk, sprightfully and bold,
Stays but the summons of the appellant's trumpet.
   Aumerle
5 Why then, the champions are prepar'd and stay
For nothing but his majesty's approach.

   The trumpets sound and King Richard
   enters with his Nobles; *when they are set,*
   enter Mowbray, the Duke of Norfolk *in*
   arms defendant

   Richard
Marshal, demand of yonder champion
The cause of his arrival here in arms.

10 *swear him*: make him swear to.

11 *say who thou art*: declare yourself; this
    was not merely formality, because the
    knight's visor would be closed and his
    face hidden.

13 *quarrel*: cause of complaint.

14 *oath*: sworn justice of the cause.

15 *so defend . . . valour*: may God and your
    courage protect you according to the
    justice of your cause.

17 *engaged*: engagèd.

18 *God defend*: God forbid.

20 *succeeding issue*: the children who
    succeed me.

21 *appeals*: accuses.

28 *plated . . . war*: clad in plate armour.

30 *Depose him*: take his deposition on oath.

34 *so . . . heaven*: so that heaven may
    defend you.

38 *lists*: the barricaded enclosure of the
    tournament.

Ask him his name, and orderly proceed
10 To swear him in the justice of his cause.
    Marshal
In God's name and the king's say who thou art,
And why thou com'st thus knightly clad in arms,
Against what man thou comest and what thy quarrel.
Speak truly on thy knighthood and thy oath,
15 And so defend thee heaven and thy valour.
    Mowbray
My name is Thomas Mowbray, Duke of Norfolk,
Who hither come engaged by my oath
(Which God defend a knight should violate)
Both to defend my loyalty and truth
20 To God, my king, and my succeeding issue,
Against the Duke of Herford that appeals me,
And by the grace of God, and this mine arm,
To prove him, in defending of myself,
A traitor to my God, my king, and me.
25 And as I truly fight, defend me heaven.

      The trumpets sound. Enter Bullingbrook,
      Duke of Herford *appellant in armour*

    Richard
Marshal, demand of yonder knight in arms
Both who he is and why he cometh hither
Thus plated in habiliments of war,
And formally according to our law
30 Depose him in the justice of his cause.
    Marshal
What is thy name? And wherefore com'st thou hither
Before King Richard in his royal lists?
Against whom comest thou, and what's thy quarrel?
Speak like a true knight, so defend thee heaven.
    Bullingbrook
35 Harry of Herford, Lancaster, and Derby
Am I, who ready here do stand in arms
To prove by God's grace and my body's valour
In lists, on Thomas Mowbray, Duke of Norfolk,
That he's a traitor foul and dangerous
40 To God of heaven, King Richard and to me;
And as I truly fight, defend me heaven.

43 *touch*: interfere in.

Marshal
On pain of death, no person be so bold
Or daring-hardy as to touch the lists,
Except the Marshal and such officers
45 Appointed to direct these fair designs.
Bullingbrook
Lord Marshal, let me kiss my sovereign's hand
And bow my knee before his majesty,
For Mowbray and myself are like two men
That vow a long and weary pilgrimage.
50 Then let us take a ceremonious leave
And loving farewell of our several friends.

51 *farewell . . . friends*: separate farewell of our different friends.

Marshal
The appellant in all duty greets your highness,
And craves to kiss your hand and take his leave.
Richard
We will descend and fold him in our arms.

54 *descend*: come down from the high chair of state *and* condescend.

55 Cousin of Herford, as thy cause is right
So be thy fortune in this royal fight.
Farewell, my blood, which if today thou shed
Lament we may, but not revenge thee dead.

58 *not revenge . . . dead*: Death of either party would indicate his guilt, so revenge could not be justified.
59 *profane a tear*: shed a false tear (which would necessarily be false if wept for a traitor).
66 *lusty*: strong, vigorous.
cheerly: cheerfully.
67 *as at English feasts*: English banquets, unlike some of those on the continent, ended with a sweet course.
regreet: salute, address.
68 *daintiest*: sweetest.
69 *thou*: Bullingbrook addresses his father, John of Gaunt.
70 *spirit*: The word is pronounced as a single syllable, 'sprite'.
regenerate: reborn, renewed.
71 *twofold*: double—i.e. both father's and son's.
lift me up: i.e. as a father lifts a child.
73 *proof*: impenetrability.
74 *steel*: strengthen.
75 *waxen coat*: i.e. as though the coat of mail were made of wax.
76 *furbish*: polish.
77 *lusty haviour*: vigorous conduct.

Bullingbrook
Oh, let no noble eye profane a tear
60 For me, if I be gor'd with Mowbray's spear.
As confident as is the falcon's flight
Against a bird do I with Mowbray fight.
My loving lord, I take my leave of you.
Of you, my noble cousin, Lord Aumerle,
65 Not sick, although I have to do with death,
But lusty, young and cheerly drawing breath.
Lo, as at English feasts so I regreet
The daintiest last, to make the end most sweet.
Oh thou, the earthly author of my blood,
70 Whose youthful spirit in me regenerate
Doth with a twofold vigour lift me up
To reach at victory above my head,
Add proof unto mine armour with thy prayers,
And with thy blessings steel my lance's point
75 That it may enter Mowbray's waxen coat,
And furbish new the name of John a Gaunt
Even in the lusty haviour of his son.

Gaunt
God in thy good cause make thee prosperous.
Be swift like lightning in the execution
80 And let thy blows, doubly redoubled,
Fall like amazing thunder on the casque
Of thy adverse pernicious enemy.
Rouse up thy youthful blood, be valiant and live.
Bullingbrook
Mine innocency and Saint George to thrive.
Mowbray
85 However God or Fortune cast my lot
There lives or dies, true to King Richard's throne,
A loyal, just and upright gentleman.
Never did captive with a freer heart
Cast off his chains of bondage and embrace
90 His golden uncontroll'd enfranchisement
More than my dancing soul doth celebrate
This feast of battle with mine adversary.
Most mighty liege and my companion peers,
Take from my mouth the wish of happy years.
95 As gentle and as jocund as to jest
Go I to fight. Truth hath a quiet breast.
Richard
Farewell, my lord. Securely I espy
Virtue with valour couched in thine eye.
Order the trial, Marshal, and begin.

81 *amazing*: bewildering.
   casque: helmet.
82 *adverse*: opposing, *and also* unfortunate.

84 *Saint George*: the patron saint of
   England.
   to thrive: I rely on for success.

90 *enfranchisement*: release from
   imprisonment.

95 *jest*: play.
96 *Truth . . . breast*: Mowbray alludes to
   the proverb, 'truth fears no trial'.

97 *Securely*: confidently.
98 *couched*: couchèd; i.e. like a lance,
   poised and ready.

101 *Receive*: The lances were measured by
the Marshal for length and weight.

102 *Strong . . . hope*: 'for thou [God] hast
been my hope, and a strong tower for
me against the enemy' (Psalm 61:3).

104 *Lancaster*: i.e. heir to the Duke of
Lancaster.

109 *him*: himself.

112 *approve*: establish.

118 *warder*: baton (held by the king or his
representative to control the
tournament).

120 *chairs*: According to Holinshed, the
chairs were canopied like pavilions,
Bullingbrook's chair in green, and
Mowbray's with red and white
damasked curtains.

121 *Withdraw with us*: Richard addresses his
order to the lords of his Council.

122 *While*: until.
return: notify.

122s.d. *A long flourish*: This 'flourish'
(= succession of trumpet calls) allows
time for the conference (which,
according to Holinshed, lasted for more
than two hours).

125 *For that*: because.

126 *fostered*: fosterèd.

127 *for*: because.

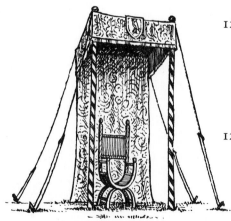

Marshal
100 Harry of Herford, Lancaster, and Derby,
Receive thy lance, and God defend the right.
    Bullingbrook
Strong as a tower in hope, I cry amen.
    Marshal
Go bear this lance to Thomas Duke of Norfolk.
    First Herald
Harry of Herford, Lancaster, and Derby
105 Stands here, for God, his sovereign and himself,
On pain to be found false and recreant,
To prove the Duke of Norfolk, Thomas Mowbray,
A traitor to his God, his king, and him,
And dares him to set forward to the fight.
    Second Herald
110 Here standeth Thomas Mowbray, Duke of Norfolk,
On pain to be found false and recreant,
Both to defend himself, and to approve
Henry of Herford, Lancaster, and Derby
To God, his sovereign, and to him disloyal,
115 Courageously and with a free desire,
Attending but the signal to begin.
    Marshal
Sound trumpets, and set forward combatants.

A charge sounded

Stay, the king hath thrown his warder down.
    Richard
Let them lay by their helmets and their spears,
120 And both return back to their chairs again.
Withdraw with us, and let the trumpets sound
While we return these dukes what we decree.

A long flourish

Draw near,
And list what with our Council we have done.
125 For that our kingdom's earth should not be soil'd
With that dear blood which it hath fostered,
And for our eyes do hate the dire aspect

128 *civil . . . sword*: injuries inflicted by
  neighbours in civil warfare.
129 *winged*: wingèd.
129–33 Shakespeare seems to have lost
  control of his images: the sleeping
  'peace' of line 132, having been
  aroused, goes on to 'fright fair peace' in
  line 137. These lines were omitted in
  Folio, perhaps because of their
  obscurity.
131 *set on you*: set you on.
132 *wake*: awaken.
133 *Draws . . . sleep*: is sleeping like a baby.
136 *shock*: impact (especially of armoured
  horses in collision).

140 *pain of life*: risk of losing your life.

142 *regreet*: greet again.

143 *stranger*: foreign.

148 *heavier doom*: more severe punishment.

150 *sly slow*: not visibly moving.
  determinate: put an end to.
151 *dateless*: endless.
  dear: grievous.

154 *heavy sentence*: i.e. not simply a
  'hopeless word'.

156 *merit*: reward.
  maim: injury.

158 *deserved*: deservèd.

159 *these forty years*: for such a long time.

162 *unstringed*: unstringèd.
  viol: A stringed instrument played with
  a bow.
163 *cunning*: ingenious, carefully made and
  requiring skill to play.
164 *his hands*: the hands of someone.
165 *knows no touch*: has no skill.

Of civil wounds plough'd up with neighbour's sword,
And for we think the eagle-winged pride
130 Of sky-aspiring and ambitious thoughts
With rival-hating envy set on you
To wake our peace, which in our country's cradle
Draws the sweet infant breath of gentle sleep,
Which so rous'd up with boisterous untun'd drums,
135 With harsh resounding trumpet's dreadful bray
And grating shock of wrathful iron arms,
Might from our quiet confines fright fair peace,
And make us wade even in our kindred's blood,
Therefore we banish you our territories.
140 You, cousin Herford, upon pain of life,
Till twice five summers have enrich'd our fields
Shall not regreet our fair dominions,
But tread the stranger paths of banishment.
       Bullingbrook
Your will be done. This must my comfort be:
145 That sun that warms you here shall shine on me,
And those his golden beams to you here lent
Shall point on me and gild my banishment.
       Richard
Norfolk, for thee remains a heavier doom,
Which I with some unwillingness pronounce.
150 The sly slow hours shall not determinate
The dateless limit of thy dear exile.
The hopeless word of never to return
Breathe I against thee, upon pain of life.
       Mowbray
A heavy sentence, my most sovereign liege,
155 And all unlook'd for from your highness' mouth.
A dearer merit, not so deep a maim
As to be cast forth in the common air,
Have I deserved at your highness' hands.
The language I have learnt these forty years,
160 My native English, now I must forgo,
And now my tongue's use is to me no more
Than an unstringed viol or a harp,
Or like a cunning instrument cas'd up,
Or being open, put into his hands
165 That knows no touch to tune the harmony.
Within my mouth you have engaol'd my tongue,

167 *portcullis'd with*: locked in behind; the 'portcullis' was an iron grille dropped down in front of a castle entrance.

170 *a nurse*: A nurse might have the responsibility for teaching her charges to speak.
174 *boots thee not*: does you no good.
be compassionate: look for sympathy.
175 *plaining*: complaining.
178 *Return again*: Richard recalls Mowbray as he turns to leave the stage.
179 *on . . . sword*: on the hilt of the sword (which, with the guard, forms a cross).

181 Richard absolves the banished men from any continuing obligation to himself.
186 *regreet*: meet again.
187 *louring*: frowning.
188 *advised purpose*: advisèd; deliberate intention.

Doubly portcullis'd with my teeth and lips,
And dull unfeeling barren ignorance
Is made my gaoler to attend on me.
170 I am too old to fawn upon a nurse,
Too far in years to be a pupil now.
What is thy sentence then but speechless death,
Which robs my tongue from breathing native breath?

    Richard
It boots thee not to be compassionate.
175 After our sentence plaining comes too late.

    Mowbray
Then thus I turn me from my country's light
To dwell in solemn shades of endless night.

    Richard
Return again, and take an oath with thee.
Lay on our royal sword your banish'd hands.
180 Swear by the duty that you owe to Gód
(Our part therein we banish with yourselves)
To keep the oath that we administer.
You never shall, so help you truth and God,
Embrace each other's love in banishment,
185 Nor never look upon each other's face,
Nor never write, regreet nor reconcile
This louring tempest of your home-bred hate,
Nor never by advised purpose meet

189 *complot*: conspire together.

To plot, contrive or complot any ill
190 'Gainst us, our state, our subjects or our land.

Bullingbrook

I swear.

Mowbray

    And I, to keep all this.

Bullingbrook

192 *so far*: let me say this.

Norfolk, so far as to mine enemy:
By this time, had the king permitted us,
One of our souls had wander'd in the air,

195 *sepulchre*: The stress is on the second syllable.

195 Banish'd this frail sepulchre of our flesh,
As now our flesh is banish'd from this land.
Confess thy treasons ere thou fly the realm.
Since thou hast far to go, bear not along

199 *clogging*: A clog was a wooden block tied to a prisoner's leg to impede his movements.
burthen: burden (an early form).
201 *My name . . . life*: Mowbray quotes the Bishops' Bible (Revelation 3:5), 'He that overcometh shall be thus clothed in white array, and I will not blot out his name out of the book of life'.
205 *no way . . . stray*: I cannot take the wrong road.
206 *Save*: except.
207 *glasses . . . eyes*: The eyes were, proverbially, the windows of the soul and heart.
208 *grieved*: grievèd.
aspect: The accent is on the second syllable.

The clogging burthen of a guilty soul.

Mowbray

200 No, Bullingbrook. If ever I were traitor,
My name be blotted from the book of life
And I from heaven banish'd as from hence.
But what thou art, God, thou and I do know,
And all too soon, I fear, the king shall rue.
205 Farewell, my liege. Now no way can I stray.
Save back to England all the world's my way.   [*Exit*

Richard

Uncle, even in the glasses of thine eyes
I see thy grieved heart. Thy sad aspect
Hath from the number of his banish'd years
210 Plucked four away. [*To* Bullingbrook] Six frozen winters spent,
Return with welcome home from banishment.

Bullingbrook

How long a time lies in one little word.
Four lagging winters and four wanton springs
End in a word, such is the breath of kings.

213 *wanton*: careless.

Gaunt

215 I thank my liege that in regard of me
He shortens four years of my son's exile;
But little vantage shall I reap thereby,
For ere the six years that he hath to spend
Can change their moons and bring their times about

219 *moons*: months.
bring . . . about: accomplish the cycles of their seasons.
221 *extinct*: extinguished.

220 My oil-dried lamp and time-bewasted light
Shall be extinct with age and endless night,

223 *blindfold Death*: Gaunt images Death as
being eyeless (like a skull) and being the
cause of sightlessness.

225 *king*: Gaunt's abrupt form of address
emphasizes both the power of Richard
and the limitations of that power.
226 *sullen*: gloomy, melancholy.
229 *his pilgrimage*: its journey.
230 *is current*: has purchasing power.
233 *a party verdict*: a share in the judgement.
234 *lour*: frown.
235 *Things . . . sour*: 'as in my mouth [it
was] sweet as honey: and as soon as I
had eaten it, my belly was bitter'
(Revelation 10:10); the expression is
proverbial.
239 *To smooth*: in glossing over.
240 *partial slander*: false accusation of being
biased.
242 *look'd when*: expected, waited for the
time when.

248 *What . . . know*: what we shall not be
able to communicate in person.

My inch of taper will be burnt and done,
And blindfold Death not let me see my son.
   Richard
Why, uncle, thou hast many years to live.
   Gaunt
225 But not a minute, king, that thou canst give.
Shorten my days thou canst with sullen sorrow,
And pluck nights from me, but not lend a morrow.
Thou canst help time to furrow me with age,
But stop no wrinkle in his pilgrimage.
230 Thy word is current with him for my death,
But dead thy kingdom cannot buy my breath.
   Richard
Thy son is banish'd upon good advice,
Whereto thy tongue a party verdict gave.
Why at our justice seemst thou then to lour?
   Gaunt
235 Things sweet to taste prove in digestion sour.
You urg'd me as a judge, but I had rather
You would have bid me argue like a father.
Oh, had it been a stranger, not my child,
To smooth his fault I should have been more mild.
240 A partial slander sought I to avoid
And in the sentence my own life destroy'd.
Alas, I look'd when some of you should say
I was too strict to make mine own away,
But you gave leave to my unwilling tongue
245 Against my will to do myself this wrong.
   Richard
Cousin, farewell, and uncle, bid him so.
Six years we banish him and he shall go.
                    [*Exit. Flourish*
   Aumerle
Cousin, farewell. What presence must not know,
From where you do remain let paper show.   [*Exit*
   Marshal
250 My lord, no leave take I, for I will ride
As far as land will let me by your side.
   Gaunt
Oh, to what purpose dost thou hoard thy words,
That thou returnst no greeting to thy friends?

255 *office*: function.
255–6 *prodigal . . . dolour*: extravagant in uttering the rich grief; Bullingbrook's pun on 'dolour' (dollar) extends the metaphor begun with 'hoard' in line 252.
257–8 *grief . . . grief*: grievance *and* cause of sorrow.

261 *travail*: Gaunt intends *both* 'labour' *and* 'travel'.
262 *miscall it so*: describe it as a journey.
263 *enforced*: enforcèd.

264 *sullen*: melancholy *and* dull in colour.
265 *foil*: defeat (in wrestling), setting (for a jewel).

268 *remember me*: remind me.
deal of world: distance.

271 *passages*: stretches of space (and time).
272 *freedom*: i.e. from his indentures (as an apprentice) *and* from exile.
273 *journeyman*: qualified artisan *and* one who has been abroad.
274–92 Gaunt delivers a string of proverbial utterances.

280 *faintly*: unwillingly.
281 *purchase*: acquire by effort.

283 *pestilence*: plague.

285 *Look what*: whatever.

Bullingbrook
I have too few to take my leave of you,
255 When the tongue's office should be prodigal
To breathe the abundant dolour of the heart.
Gaunt
Thy grief is but thy absence for a time.
Bullingbrook
Joy absent, grief is present for that time.
Gaunt
What is six winters? They are quickly gone.
Bullingbrook
260 To men in joy; but grief makes one hour ten.
Gaunt
Call it a travail that thou tak'st for pleasure.
Bullingbrook
My heart will sigh when I miscall it so,
Which finds it an enforced pilgrimage.
Gaunt
The sullen passage of thy weary steps
265 Esteem as foil wherein thou art to set
The precious jewel of thy home return.
Bullingbrook
Nay, rather every tedious stride I make
Will but remember me what a deal of world
I wander from the jewels that I love.
270 Must I not serve a long apprenticehood
To foreign passages, and in the end,
Having my freedom, boast of nothing else
But that I was a journeyman to grief?
Gaunt
All places that the eye of heaven visits
275 Are to a wise man ports and happy havens.
Teach thy necessity to reason thus:
There is no virtue like necessity.
Think not the king did banish thee,
But thou the king. Woe doth the heavier sit
280 Where it perceives it is but faintly borne.
Go, say I sent thee forth to purchase honour,
And not the king exil'd thee; or suppose
Devouring pestilence hangs in our air
And thou art flying to a fresher clime.
285 Look what thy soul holds dear, imagine it

To lie that way thou goest, not whence thou com'st.
Suppose the singing birds musicians,
The grass whereon thou treadst the presence strew'd,
The flowers fair ladies, and thy steps no more
290 Than a delightful measure or a dance,
For gnarling sorrow hath less power to bite
The man that mocks at it and sets it light.

Bullingbrook
Oh, who can hold a fire in his hand
By thinking on the frosty Caucasus?
295 Or cloy the hungry edge of appetite
By bare imagination of a feast?
Or wallow naked in December snow
By thinking on fantastic summer's heat?
Oh no, the apprehension of the good
300 Gives but the greater feeling to the worse.
Fell Sorrow's tooth doth never rankle more
Than when he bites but lanceth not the sore.

Gaunt
Come, come, my son, I'll bring thee on thy way.
Had I thy youth and cause I would not stay.

Bullingbrook
305 Then England's ground farewell, sweet soil adieu,
My mother and my nurse that bears me yet.
Where'er I wander, boast of this I can,
Though banish'd, yet a true born Englishman.
[*Exeunt*

---

288 *the presence strew'd*: the royal presence chamber with rushes strewn on the floor.
290 *measure*: stately dance.
291 *gnarling*: gnashing *and* snarling.
292 *sets it light*: takes it lightly.

294 *frosty Caucasus*: The high mountain range was perpetually frozen.
295 *cloy*: surfeit, satisfy to excess.

298 *fantastic*: imaginary.
299 *apprehension*: conception, understanding.

301 *Fell*: cruel.
302 *lanceth . . . sore*: makes no open wound to release the poison inside—i.e. like a snake or mosquito.
303 *bring thee*: accompany you.
304 *stay*: delay.

Act I   Scene 4

Richard hears of the departure of Bullingbrook into exile. As he is making plans to raise money for the wars in Ireland, he learns about the sickness of John of Gaunt.

1 *We did observe*: The king enters in the middle of a conversation.
2 *high*: proud, mighty. The irony of this single adjective disperses the (apparent) impartiality of the previous scenes.
4 *next*: nearest.

Scene 4

The Court. Enter King Richard *with* Green *and* Bagot *at one door, and the* Lord Aumerle *at another*

Richard
We did observe. Cousin Aumerle,
How far brought you high Herford on his way?

Aumerle
I brought high Herford, if you call him so,
But to the next highway, and there I left him.

Richard

5 And say, what store of parting tears were shed?

Aumerle

Faith, none for me, except the northeast wind,
Which then blew bitterly against our faces,
Awak'd the sleeping rheum and so by chance
Did grace our hollow parting with a tear.

Richard

10 What said our cousin when you parted with him?

Aumerle

'Farewell',
And, for my heart disdained that my tongue
Should so profane the word, that taught me craft
To counterfeit oppression of such grief
15 That words seemed buried in my sorrow's grave.
Marry, would the word 'farewell' have lengthen'd
   hours
And added years to his short banishment,
He should have had a volume of 'farewells'.
But since it would not he had none of me.

Richard

20 He is our cousin, cousin, but 'tis doubt,
When time shall call him home from banishment,
Whether our kinsman come to see his friends.
Our self and Bushy, Bagot here and Green,
Observ'd his courtship to the common people,
25 How he did seem to dive into their hearts
With humble and familiar courtesy,
What reverence he did throw away on slaves,
Wooing poor craftsmen with the craft of smiles
And patient underbearing of his fortune,
30 As 'twere to banish their affects with him.
Off goes his bonnet to an oysterwench.
A brace of draymen bid God speed him well
And had the tribute of his supple knee,
With 'Thanks, my countrymen, my loving friends',
35 As were our England in reversion his,
And he our subjects' next degree in hope.

Green

Well, he is gone, and with him go these thoughts.
Now, for the rebels which stand out in Ireland,
Expedient manage must be made, my liege,

6 *for me*: on my part.

8 *rheum*: A watery discharge from eyes and nose.
9 *hollow*: insincere.

11 *'Farewell'*: The short line emphasizes the abruptness of the parting.
12 *for*: because.
   disdained: disdainèd.
13 *that*: i.e. the disdainful heart.
14 *counterfeit*: pretend to.
15 *words*: i.e. any more words (besides 'Farewell').

18 *volume*: bookful.

20 *cousin, cousin*: Richard, Aumerle, and Bullingbrook were all related as cousins (see 'Family Tree', p. vi–vii).
20–2 *'tis doubt . . . come*: Richard's 'doubt' hints a threat to Bullingbrook.

27 *reverence*: respectfulness.

29 *underbearing*: endurance.
30 *banish . . . with him*: take their affections into banishment with them.
33 *supple*: easily bending (to make a bow).
35 *As were . . . his*: as though he were next heir to my country; 'in reversion' is the legal term for a coming inheritance.
36 *next . . . hope*: next in the line of inheritance for our subjects' expectations; Richard had already named the son of Roger Mortimer as his successor—see 'Family Tree', p. vi–vii.
38 *stand out*: are holding out in resistance.
39 *Expedient manage*: suitably prompt organization.

40 Ere further leisure yield them further means
For their advantage and your highness' loss.
  Richard
We will ourself in person to this war,
And, for our coffers, with too great a court
And liberal largesse, are grown somewhat light,
45 We are enforc'd to farm our royal realm,
The revenue whereof shall furnish us
For our affairs in hand. If that come short
Our substitutes at home shall have blank charters
Whereto when they shall know what men are rich
50 They shall subscribe them for large sums of gold
And send them after to supply our wants,
For we will make for Ireland presently.

       Enter Bushy

Bushy, what news?
  Bushy
Old John of Gaunt is grievous sick, my lord,
55 Suddenly taken, and hath sent post haste
To entreat your majesty to visit him.
  Richard
Where lies he?
  Bushy
         At Ely House.
  Richard
Now put it, God, in the physician's mind
To help him to his grave immediately.
60 The lining of his coffers shall make coats
To deck our soldiers for these Irish wars.
Come, gentlemen, let's all go visit him.
Pray God we may make haste and come too late.
  All
Amen.   [*Exeunt*

---

43 *for*: because.
   too great a court: excessive entertainment at court.
44 *liberal largesse*: generous grants and donations.
45–50 *farm . . . gold*: Shakespeare owes these details, and the phraseology of these lines, to the anonymous play *Woodstock*; see 'Shakespeare's Sources', p. 108.
45 *farm*: lease out; Richard allotted sections of the country to tax-farmers, who then had the right to extort their own taxes from the people.
48 *substitutes*: deputies.
   blank charters: i.e. blank cheques, which the wealthy would be compelled to sign.
50 *subscribe them*: put them down for.
52 *presently*: immediately.

57 *Ely House*: The London palace of the Bishops of Ely, which was often rented out to the nobility.

60 *lining*: contents; Richard puns on the secondary meaning (= cloth lining).

64 *Amen*: Richard's followers respond to his prayer.

Act 2

Act 2   Scene 1

John of Gaunt, dying, speaks about the state
of the nation and gives Richard a warning.
Richard is unmoved. Gaunt leaves the
stage—soon we hear that he is dead. The
king, refusing to hear York's remonstrances,
seizes all Gaunt's wealth (which Bullingbrook
should inherit), and sets out for Ireland.
Discontented nobles criticize, and speak
warmly of Bullingbrook. Northumberland
has news.

2 *unstaid*: uncontrolled.

10 *glose*: talk superficially, prattle on.

12 *music at the close*: the final cadences of a
   piece of music.

14 *Writ in remembrance*: remembered.

16 *death's sad tale*: serious last words.

18 *the . . . fond*: Gaunt seems to be ironic.

19 *metres*: verses.
   venom: poisonous.

22 *apish*: imitative.

Scene 1

> *Ely House. Enter* John of Gaunt, *sick, with*
> *the* Duke of York, *etc.*

Gaunt
Will the king come that I may breathe my last
In wholesome counsel to his unstaid youth?
York
Vex not yourself, nor strive not with your breath,
For all in vain comes counsel to his ear.
Gaunt
5 Oh, but they say the tongues of dying men
Enforce attention like deep harmony.
Where words are scarce they are seldom spent in
   vain,
For they breathe truth that breathe their words in
   pain.
He that no more must say is listen'd more
10 Than they whom youth and ease have taught to
   glose.
More are men's ends mark'd than their lives before.
The setting sun, and music at the close,
As the last taste of sweets, is sweetest last,
Writ in remembrance more than things long past.
15 Though Richard my life's counsel would not hear
My death's sad tale may yet undeaf his ear.
York
No, it is stopp'd with other flattering sounds,
As praises, of whose taste the wise are fond,
Lascivious metres, to whose venom sound
20 The open ear of youth doth always listen,
Report of fashions in proud Italy,
Whose manners still our tardy-apish nation

25 *So*: provided that.
  there's no respect: it doesn't matter.
28 *will . . . regard*: passion rebels with the consent of reason (which ought to control the passion).
31 *inspir'd*: Gaunt picks up York's advice to save his breath, retorting that new life has been breathed into him.
32 *expiring*: dying *and* breathing out.
33–7 The sentiments in these lines are all more or less proverbial.
36 *betimes . . . betimes*: very quickly . . . too early.
38 *insatiate cormorant*: This bird of prey is proverbially a greedy feeder.
41 *earth of majesty*: land which is the seat for kingship.
  Mars: the god of war (in classical mythology).
42 *other Eden*: second paradise.
44 *infection . . . war*. Gaunt may be thinking of the so-called 'Hundred Years War' (1338–1360), but Shakespeare and his audiences would remember the threat of the Spanish Armada (1588) and also the civil wars that had plagued France for the past thirty years.
45 *happy breed*: fortunate race.
47 *office*: function.
50 *blessed*: blessèd.
51 *teeming*: fertile.
52 *Fear'd by*: inspiring fear by.
53 *Renowned*: renownèd.
53–5 *deeds . . . Jewry*: Gaunt thinks of crusaders such as Richard I and Edward I who fought to protect the Christian shrines in Jerusalem.
55 *stubborn Jewry*: the homeland of the stubborn Jews (who resisted both Christ and, later, the crusaders).
56 *world's ransom . . . son*: Christians believe that Christ (whose mother was the Virgin Mary) died to redeem the world from its sins.
  blessed: blessèd.
57–8 *dear*. The repetition of the word (whose meanings include 'beloved', 'expensive', and 'invaluable') prepares for the monstrosity of the deed to be described.
59 *leas'd out*: See *1, 4, 45–50* and 'Shakespeare's Sources', p. 108.

Limps after in base imitation.
Where doth the world thrust forth a vanity—
25 So it be new there's no respect how vile—
That is not quickly buzz'd into his ears?
Then all too late comes counsel to be heard
Where will doth mutiny with wit's regard.
Direct not him whose way himself will choose.
30 'Tis breath thou lackst and that breath wilt thou lose.
       Gaunt
Methinks I am a prophet new inspir'd,
And thus expiring do foretell of him.
His rash fierce blaze of riot cannot last,
For violent fires soon burn out themselves.
35 Small showers last long but sudden storms are short.
He tires betimes that spurs too fast betimes.
With eager feeding food doth choke the feeder.
Light vanity, insatiate cormorant,
Consuming means, soon preys upon itself.
40 This royal throne of kings, this sceptred isle,
This earth of majesty, this seat of Mars,
This other Eden, demi-paradise,
This fortress built by Nature for herself
Against infection and the hand of war,
45 This happy breed of men, this little world,
This precious stone set in the silver sea
Which serves it in the office of a wall
Or as a moat defensive to a house
Against the envy of less happier lands,
50 This blessed plot, this earth, this realm, this England,
This nurse, this teeming womb of royal kings
Fear'd by their breed and famous by their birth,
Renowned for their deeds as far from home
For Christian service and true chivalry
55 As is the sepulchre in stubborn Jewry
Of the world's ransom, blessed Mary's son,
This land of such dear souls, this dear, dear land,
Dear for her reputation through the world,
Is now leas'd out, I die pronouncing it,

60 *tenement*: property held by a tenant.
   pelting farm: smallholding, allotment;
   the phrase ('pelting' = paltry) is from
   Woodstock.

61–3 *bound in . . . bound in*: surrounded by
   . . . legally restrained by.

62 *siege*: assault.

64 *inky blots . . . bonds*: The visual image
   emphasizes the shabbiness of the
   dealings.

65 *wont*: accustomed.

67 *would*: if only.

69 *The king is come*: Probably a fanfare on
   the trumpets would herald the entrance
   of the king and his company.

70 *rein'd*: reined back, held in.

72 *aged*: agèd.

73 *composition*: condition, state both of
   mind and body.

75 *grief . . . fast*: A fast was often observed
   as an expression of grief.

76 *meat*: food.

77 *sleeping England*: i.e. both the country
   and its monarch.
   watch'd: kept awake, kept guard.

78 *Watching*: lack of sleep.
   all gaunt: completely haggard *and*
   'Gaunt' entirely.

80 *Is my strict fast*: that which I must go
   without.
   my children's looks: the sight of my
   children.

83 *inherits*: receives as its due.

84 *so nicely*: with such subtle triviality.

85 *misery . . . itself*: wretchedness takes
   pleasure in ridiculing itself.

86 *to kill . . . in me*: i.e. by banishing his
   son.

87 *flatter*: deceive, delude; the word has
   many variations of meaning.

88 *flatter with*: try to please.

60 Like to a tenement or pelting farm.
    England, bound in with the triumphant sea
    Whose rocky shore beats back the envious siege
    Of watery Neptune, is now bound in with shame,
    With inky blots and rotten parchment bonds,
65 That England that was wont to conquer others
    Hath made a shameful conquest of itself.
    Ah, would the scandal vanish with my life,
    How happy then were my ensuing death!

   Enter King Richard, Queen, Aumerle,
   Bushy, Green, Bagot, Ross, *and*
   Willoughby

   York
    The king is come. Deal mildly with his youth,
70 For young hot colts being rein'd do rage the more.
   Queen
    How fares our noble uncle Lancaster?
   Richard
    What comfort, man? How is't with aged Gaunt?
   Gaunt
    Oh, how that name befits my composition!
    Old Gaunt indeed, and gaunt in being old.
75 Within me grief hath kept a tedious fast,
    And who abstains from meat that is not gaunt?
    For sleeping England long time have I watch'd.
    Watching breeds leanness; leanness is all gaunt.
    The pleasure that some fathers feed upon
80 Is my strict fast, I mean my children's looks,
    And therein fasting hast thou made me gaunt.
    Gaunt am I for the grave, gaunt as a grave,
    Whose hollow womb inherits naught but bones.
   Richard
    Can sick men play so nicely with their names?
   Gaunt
85 No, misery makes sport to mock itself.
    Since thou dost seek to kill my name in me
    I mock my name, great king, to flatter thee.
   Richard
    Should dying men flatter with those that live?
   Gaunt
    No, no, men living flatter those that die.

92 *see thee ill*: see that you are sick.
93 *see thee ill*: Gaunt picks up Richard's
     words and plays with different meanings
     (= see you imperfectly, see you are sick,
     see evil in you).
97 *too careless patient*: i.e. too careless about
     your health *and* too casual in permitting
     wrong.
98 *anointed body*: Richard's body was
     anointed with holy oil at his coronation
     (see *1, 2, 38*).
     cure: treatment.
99 *physicians*: i.e. Richard's flattering
     favourites.
101 *compass*: boundary.
102 *encaged*: encagèd.
     verge: bound (including senses of
     'compass', 'sphere of jurisdiction',
     'measure of land').

103 *waste*: damage (with a pun on 'waist').
104 *thy grandsire*: Edward III.
105 *destroy his sons*: The syntax allows two
     senses—*both* 'the sons of Edward III'
     and 'Richard's own descendants'.
107 *Deposing*: disinheriting.
     wert possess'd: took possession (of the
     kingdom).
108 *art possess'd*: madness, possessed by the
     devil.
109 *regent*: governor.
111 *for thy world . . . land*: since the only
     world you have is this country.
114 *Thy state . . . law*: By leasing out his
     kingdom, Richard has made the king
     subject to the law (Gaunt believes that
     the monarch, as law-giver, should be
     above the law).
115 Richard turns the sentence back on
     Gaunt (perhaps saying 'thou'
     simultaneously with him).
     lean-witted: feeble-minded ('gaunt' in
     mind as well as body).
116 *ague's privilege*: allowance for the
     feverishly sick.
117 *frozen*: ice-cold; the ague was
     characterized by alternate bouts of
     shivering and sweating.

Richard
90 Thou now a-dying sayest thou flatterest me.
       Gaunt
     Oh no, thou diest, though I the sicker be.
       Richard
     I am in health, I breathe, and see thee ill.
       Gaunt
     Now He that made me knows I see thee ill,
     Ill in myself to see, and in thee, seeing ill.
95 Thy deathbed is no lesser than thy land,
     Wherein thou liest in reputation sick,
     And thou, too careless patient as thou art,
     Commit'st thy anointed body to the cure
     Of those physicians that first wounded thee.
100 A thousand flatterers sit within thy crown
     Whose compass is no bigger than thy head,
     And yet encaged in so small a verge
     The waste is no whit lesser than thy land.
     Oh, had thy grandsire with a prophet's eye
105 Seen how his son's son should destroy his sons,
     From forth thy reach he would have laid thy shame,
     Deposing thee before thou wert possess'd,
     Which art possess'd now to depose thyself.
     Why, cousin, wert thou regent of the world
110 It were a shame to let this land by lease,
     But for thy world enjoying but this land
     Is it not more than shame to shame it so?
     Landlord of England art thou now, not king,
     Thy state of law is bondslave to the law,
115 And thou—
       Richard
              A lunatic lean-witted fool,
     Presuming on an ague's privilege,
     Dar'st with thy frozen admonition

120 *my seat*: i.e. my state of law.
121 *great Edward's son*: i.e. the Black Prince, Richard's father.
122 *roundly*: freely, bluntly.
123 *unreverent*: disrespectful, not bowed in respect.
124 *brother Edward*: i.e. Edward the Black Prince.
125 *his father Edward*: Edward III.
126 *pelican*: The bird (emblem both of parental care and filial ingratitude) was thought to feed its young with blood pecked from its own breast.

127 *tapp'd out*: drawn like a drink from a barrel.
128 *plain well-meaning soul*: Shakespeare's Duke of Gloucester is based on the Gloucester of *Woodstock* rather than the historical figure.
129 *fair befall*: may good befall.
130 *May be*: must be; Gaunt openly accuses Richard of the murder of Gloucester.
precedent: example, proof.
131 *thou respect'st not*: you have no scruples about.
133 *unkindness*: unnatural behaviour.
be: will be.
135 *die . . . thee*: may your ill reputation live after you.
137 *Convey*: carry, escort.
139 *sullens*: sulks.
140 *become*: are fitting for.
143–4 *dear . . . Herford*: as dearly as he loves his son Hereford (Bullingbrook); Richard chooses to interpret 'as dearly as Hereford loves Richard'.

Make pale our cheek, chasing the royal blood
With fury from his native residence.
120 Now, by my seat's right royal majesty,
Wert thou not brother to great Edward's son
This tongue that runs so roundly in thy head
Should run thy head from thy unreverent shoulders.
    Gaunt
Oh spare me not, my brother Edward's son,
125 For that I was his father Edward's son.
That blood already, like the pelican,
Hast thou tapp'd out and drunkenly carous'd.
My brother Gloucester, plain well-meaning soul,
Whom fair befall in heaven 'mongst happy souls,
130 May be a precedent and witness good
That thou respect'st not spilling Edward's blood.
Join with the present sickness that I have
And thy unkindness be like crooked age
To crop at once a too long wither'd flower.
135 Live in thy shame, but die not shame with thee.
These words hereafter thy tormentors be.
Convey me to my bed, then to my grave.
Love they to live that love and honour have.   [*Exit*
    Richard
And let them die that age and sullens have,
140 For both hast thou, and both become the grave.
    York
I do beseech your majesty, impute his words
To wayward sickliness and age in him.
He loves you, on my life, and holds you dear
As Harry Duke of Herford were he here.
    Richard
145 Right, you say true. As Herford's love, so his.
As theirs, so mine, and all be as it is.

Enter Northumberland

    Northumberland
My liege, old Gaunt commends him to your majesty.
    Richard
What says he?
    Northumberland
        Nay nothing, all is said.

149 *stringless instrument*: The image recalls
    that used by Mowbray at *1*, 3, 161–2.
150 *spent*: ended, expended; York takes up
    the financial image in the next lines.
152 *death*: i.e. the state of being dead.
154 *pilgrimage*: journey through life.
    must be: must continue, *or* must also
    come to an end.
155 *Irish wars*: See *1*, 4, 60–1.
156 *rug-headed*: shaggy-haired.
    kern: foot soldiers.

157 *venom*: i.e. snakes.
157–8 *where . . . live*: Legend has it that
    snakes were driven out of Ireland by
    St Patrick.
159 *ask some charge*: call for considerable
    expenditure.
160 *seize*: take legal possession of.
162 *stand possess'd*: owned by right.
166 *Gaunt's rebukes*: i.e. the rebukes and
    insults offered to Gaunt by Richard in
    lines 115–23.
    private wrongs: wrongs done to private
    individuals.
167–8 *prevention . . . marriage*: Richard had
    forestalled a move to marry
    Bullingbrook to a cousin of the French
    king.
168 *my own disgrace*: The play *Woodstock* is
    the only known source for this detail:
    Gloucester, speaking to York and
    Lancaster, says that Richard has
    'disgraced our names and thrust us
    from his court'.
170 *bend one wrinkle on*: turn a single frown
    upon.
171 *last*: last surviving.

His tongue is now a stringless instrument.
150 Words, life and all old Lancaster hath spent.
    York
    Be York the next that must be bankrupt so.
    Though death be poor it ends a mortal woe.
    Richard
    The ripest fruit first falls, and so doth he.
    His time is spent, our pilgrimage must be.
155 So much for that. Now, for our Irish wars,
    We must supplant those rough rug-headed kern,
    Which live like venom where no venom else
    But only they have privilege to live.
    And, for these great affairs do ask some charge,
160 Towards our assistance we do seize to us
    The plate, coin, revenues, and moveables
    Whereof our uncle Gaunt did stand possess'd.
    York
    How long shall I be patient? Ah, how long
    Shall tender duty make me suffer wrong?
165 Not Gloucester's death nor Herford's banishment,
    Nor Gaunt's rebukes, nor England's private wrongs,
    Nor the prevention of poor Bullingbrook
    About his marriage, nor my own disgrace
    Have ever made me sour my patient cheek
170 Or bend one wrinkle on my sovereign's face.
    I am the last of noble Edward's sons,
    Of whom thy father, Prince of Wales, was first.

177 *Accomplish'd . . . hours*: when he was
    your age.
182 *His . . . blood*: Now York, like Gaunt at
    line 131, speaks openly about the
    murder of Gloucester.
189 *gripe*: grasp.
190 *royalties*: rights granted by the monarch
    to a subject.
    rights: prerogatives that accompany
    royal blood.
195 *rights*: i.e. of inheritance and succession.
    time: time-honoured tradition.
196 *His*: Time's.
197 *ensue*: follow.
198 *thyself*: i.e. a king.
199 *sequence*: order, progression.
202-4 *Call in . . . homage*: Under feudal law,
    Gaunt's lands would revert to the
    monarch until the heir could prove his
    title and pay his homage to the king; the
    exiled Bullingbrook could have
    proceeded by attorney—but Richard
    has withdrawn this privilege.
    Call in: revoke.
    letters patents: open letters of permission.

203-4 *sue . . . livery*: institute proceedings
    for the possession of his father's lands.

206 *disposed*: disposèd.

In war was never lion rag'd more fierce,
In peace was never gentle lamb more mild
175 Than was that young and princely gentleman.
His face thou hast, for even so look'd he,
Accomplish'd with the number of thy hours.
But when he frown'd it was against the French
And not against his friends. His noble hand
180 Did win what he did spend, and spent not that
Which his triumphant father's hand had won.
His hands were guilty of no kindred blood
But bloody with the enemies of his kin.
Oh, Richard! York is too far gone with grief,
185 Or else he never would compare between.
    Richard
Why, uncle, what's the matter?
    York
                    O my liege,
Pardon me if you please; if not, I, pleas'd
Not to be pardon'd, am content with all.
Seek you to seize and gripe into your hands
190 The royalties and rights of banish'd Herford?
Is not Gaunt dead? And doth not Herford live?
Was not Gaunt just? And is not Harry true?
Did not the one deserve to have an heir?
Is not his heir a well-deserving son?
195 Take Herford's rights away and take from time
His charters and his customary rights.
Let not tomorrow then ensue today.
Be not thyself. For how art thou a king
But by fair sequence and succession?
200 Now, afore God—God forbid I say true—
If you do wrongfully seize Herford's rights,
Call in the letters patents that he hath
By his attorneys-general to sue
His livery, and deny his offer'd homage,
205 You pluck a thousand dangers on your head,
You lose a thousand well-disposed hearts,
And prick my tender patience to those thoughts
Which honour and allegiance cannot think.
    Richard
Think what you will, we seize into our hands
210 His plate, his goods, his money, and his lands.

York

I'll not be by the while. My liege, farewell.

What will ensue hereof there's none can tell,

But by bad courses may be understood

That their events can never fall out good.   [*Exit*

Richard

215 Go, Bushy, to the Earl of Wiltshire straight.

Bid him repair to us to Ely House

To see this business. Tomorrow next

We will for Ireland, and 'tis time, I trow.

And we create in absence of ourself

220 Our uncle York lord governor of England,

For he is just, and always lov'd us well.

Come on, our queen; tomorrow must we part.

Be merry, for our time of stay is short.

[*Exeunt* King Richard *and* Queen,

Aumerle, Bushy, Green, *and* Bagot

Northumberland

Well, lords, the Duke of Lancaster is dead.

Ross

225 And living too, for now his son is duke.

Willoughby

Barely in title, not in revenues.

Northumberland

Richly in both if justice had her right.

Ross

My heart is great, but it must break with silence

Ere't be disburden'd with a liberal tongue.

Northumberland

230 Nay, speak thy mind, and let him ne'er speak more

That speaks thy words again to do thee harm.

Willoughby

Tends that that thou wouldst speak to the Duke of

Herford?

If it be so, out with it boldly, man.

Quick is mine ear to hear of good towards him.

Ross

235 No good at all that I can do for him,

Unless you call it good to pity him,

Bereft, and gelded of his patrimony.

211 *by the while*: present for this.

214 *events*: consequences.

216 *repair*: make his way to.
217 *see*: organize.
   Tomorrow next: this next morning.
218 *'tis . . . trow*: I think it is high time.

228 *great*: swollen with emotion.
   with silence: with keeping silent.
229 *liberal tongue*: free speech.

232 *Tends*: pertains.

237 *gelded*: castrated, cut off from.

239 *mo*: more.

241–2 *The king . . . flatterers*: This is the
charge levelled against the king in
Woodstock—and also against Elizabeth I.
243 *Merely*: purely.
244 *prosecute*: take action against.

246 *pill'd*: despoiled; *Woodstock* refers to
'these that pill (= rob) the poor, to jet
in gold'.
248 *ancient*: long-standing.

249 *exactions*: taxes.

250 *blanks*: blank charters; see *1, 4,* 48 and
note.
benevolences: forced loans.
wot: know.
251 *this*: i.e. all this new income.
252 *Wars hath*: The singular form of the
verb with plural subject is not
uncommon in Elizabethan English.
253–4 *basely . . . blows*: Richard in 1397
surrendered the port of Brest, to the
disgust of Gloucester (Woodstock).
256 *in farm*: farmed out, leased out (see
1, 4, 45 and 'Shakespeare's Sources',
p. 108).
257 *broken man*: an ordinary bankrupt.
258 *dissolution*: dissipation, bankruptcy.

262 *degenerate*: i.e. morally inferior to his
ancestors (specifically Edward III and
the Black Prince).
266 *strike not*: i.e. don't take precautions;
the term is nautical, meaning 'reduce
sails'.
securely: in the overconfident illusion of
security.

268 *unavoided*: impossible to avoid.
269 *suffering*: allowing.

Northumberland
Now afore God 'tis shame such wrongs are borne
In him, a royal prince, and many mo
240 Of noble blood in this declining land.
The king is not himself, but basely led
By flatterers, and what they will inform
Merely in hate 'gainst any of us all
That will the king severely prosecute
245 'Gainst us, our lives, our children, and our heirs.
Ross
The commons hath he pill'd with grievous taxes
And quite lost their hearts. The nobles hath he fin'd
For ancient quarrels and quite lost their hearts.
Willoughby
And daily new exactions are devis'd,
250 As blanks, benevolences, and I wot not what.
But what a God's name doth become of this?
Northumberland
Wars hath not wasted it, for warr'd he hath not,
But basely yielded upon compromise
That which his ancestors achiev'd with blows.
255 More hath he spent in peace than they in wars.
Ross
The Earl of Wiltshire hath the realm in farm.
Willoughby
The king grown bankrupt like a broken man.
Northumberland
Reproach and dissolution hangeth over him.
Ross
He hath not money for these Irish wars,
260 His burthenous taxations notwithstanding,
But by the robbing of the banish'd duke.
Northumberland
His noble kinsman, most degenerate king!
But lords, we hear this fearful tempest sing
Yet seek no shelter to avoid the storm.
265 We see the wind sit sore upon our sails
And yet we strike not but securely perish.
Ross
We see the very wreck that we must suffer,
And unavoided is the danger now
For suffering so the causes of our wreck.

270–1 *through . . . peering*: even in death I can see the hope of new life.

270 *hollow eyes*: empty eye-sockets (of a skull).

272 *tidings*: news, information.

275 *thy self*: as one with you.

277–88 The names are taken from Holinshed.

278 *Brittaine*: Brittany, Bretagne.
intelligence: information, news.

280 *The son . . . Arundel*: This line was omitted in some early editions, possibly because Queen Elizabeth had executed another Earl of Arundel in 1595.

281 *late*: recently.

282 *His brother*: i.e. Arundel's brother.

285 *furnish'd*: equipped.

286 *tall*: large, grand.
three thousand . . . war: The number of Bullingbrook's followers had to be estimated (some historians say 'not past fifteen lances'); Shakespeare takes the largest of the estimates.

289 *stay*: wait for.

290 *The . . . king*: the king to depart first.

292 *Imp out*: mend and strengthen (as a falcon's wing is repaired by the insertion of new feathers).

293 *broking pawn*: pawnbroking; Northumberland picks up the image from Willoughby's 'broken man' of line 257.

294 *gilt*: gold leaf; Northumberland also offers a pun with 'guilt'.

296 *in post*: in haste.
Ravenspurgh: A port on the Humber, now under the sea.

297 *faint*: hesitate.

299 *Urge*: recommend.

300 *Hold out my horse*: assuming my horse holds out.

Northumberland
270 Not so. Even through the hollow eyes of death
I spy life peering, but I dare not say
How near the tidings of our comfort is.
   Willoughby
Nay, let us share thy thoughts as thou dost ours.
   Ross
Be confident to speak, Northumberland.
275 We three are but thy self, and speaking so
Thy words are but as thoughts. Therefore be bold.
   Northumberland
Then thus: I have from le Port Blanc,
A bay in Brittaine, receiv'd intelligence
That Harry Duke of Herford, Rainold Lord
   Cobham,
280 The son of Richard Earl of Arundel,
That late broke from the Duke of Exeter,
His brother, Archbishop late of Canterbury,
Sir Thomas Erpingham, Sir John Ramston,
Sir John Norbery, Sir Robert Waterton, and Francis
   Coint,
285 All these well furnish'd by the Duke of Brittaine
With eight tall ships, three thousand men of war,
Are making hither with all due expedience
And shortly mean to touch our northern shore.
Perhaps they had ere this, but that they stay
290 The first departing of the king for Ireland.
If then we shall shake off our slavish yoke,
Imp out our drooping country's broken wing,
Redeem from broking pawn the blemish'd crown,
Wipe off the dust that hides our sceptre's gilt,
295 And make high majesty look like itself,
Away with me in post to Ravenspurgh.
But if you faint, as fearing to do so,
Stay and be secret, and myself will go.
   Ross
To horse, to horse! Urge doubts to them that fear.
   Willoughby
300 Hold out my horse, and I will first be there. [*Exeunt*

Act 2   Scene 2

The queen fears unknown danger; Bushy
attempts to comfort her, but Green brings
news of Bullingbrook's return from exile.
York, already confused, learns of his son's
absence, the death of the Duchess of
Gloucester, and Bullingbrook's arrival in
England. Bushy, Bagot, and Green make
their own decisions.

2 *with*: from.
3 *life-harming heaviness*: The Elizabethans
   believed that a drop of blood was
   consumed with every sigh.

14 *Each substance . . . shadows*: for each real
    cause of grief there are twenty
    imaginary ones.
16 *glazed*: glazèd.
17 *entire*: complete in itself.
18 *perspectives*: The word is pronounced
    with stress on first and third syllables.
    Bushy describes a kind of painting
    popular in the sixteenth century (e.g.
    Holbein's 'The Ambassadors') where
    different perspectives confuse the eye.
    rightly: from the front, in the normal
    manner.

19 *awry*: obliquely.

21 *Looking awry*: misjudging,
    misinterpreting.
22 *himself*: the original grief.
    wail: bewail, weep for.

25 *More than . . . not*: don't weep for
    anything except your husband's
    departure.

27 *for*: instead of.
    weeps: weeps for.

Scene 2

Windsor Castle. Enter the Queen, Bushy,
Bagot

   Bushy
Madam, your majesty is too much sad.
You promis'd, when you parted with the king,
To lay aside life-harming heaviness
And entertain a cheerful disposition.
   Queen
5 To please the king I did. To please myself
I cannot do it; yet I know no cause
Why I should welcome such a guest as grief
Save bidding farewell to so sweet a guest
As my sweet Richard. Yet again methinks
10 Some unborn sorrow ripe in Fortune's womb
Is coming towards me, and my inward soul
With nothing trembles; at some thing it grieves,
More than with parting from my lord the king.
   Bushy
Each substance of a grief hath twenty shadows
15 Which shows like grief itself but is not so,
For sorrow's eye, glazed with blinding tears,
Divides one thing entire to many objects,
Like perspectives, which rightly gaz'd upon

Show nothing but confusion; eyed awry
20 Distinguish form. So your sweet majesty,
Looking awry upon your lord's departure,
Find shapes of grief more than himself to wail
Which, look'd on as it is, is naught but shadows
Of what it is not. Then, thrice-gracious queen,
25 More than your lord's departure weep not. More's
    not seen,
Or if it be 'tis with false sorrow's eye
Which for things true weeps things imaginary.

Queen
It may be so, but yet my inward soul
Persuades me it is otherwise. Howe'er it be
30 I cannot but be sad, so heavy sad
As, though on thinking on no thought I think,
Makes me with heavy nothing faint and shrink.
　Bushy
'Tis nothing but conceit, my gracious lady.
　Queen
'Tis nothing less. Conceit is still deriv'd
35 From some forefather grief. Mine is not so,
For nothing hath begot my something grief,
Or something hath the nothing that I grieve.
'Tis in reversion that I do possess,
But what it is that is not yet known what
40 I cannot name; 'tis nameless woe I wot.

Enter Green

　Green
God save your majesty, and well met, gentlemen.
I hope the king is not yet shipp'd for Ireland.
　Queen
Why hopest thou so? 'Tis better hope he is,
For his designs crave haste, his haste good hope;
45 Then wherefore dost thou hope he is not shipp'd?
　Green
That he, our hope, might have retir'd his power
And driven into despair an enemy's hope
Who strongly hath set footing in this land.
The banish'd Bullingbrook repeals himself
50 And with uplifted arms is safe arriv'd
At Ravenspurgh.
　Queen
　　　　　　　　　Now God in heaven forbid!
　Green
Ah, madam, 'tis too true; and that is worse
The Lord Northumberland, his son young Harry
　　Percy,
The lords of Ross, Beaumond, and Willoughby,
55 With all their powerful friends are fled to him.
　Bushy
Why have you not proclaim'd Northumberland
And all the rest, revolted faction, traitors?

30–2 *so heavy . . . shrink*: The queen indulges her depression in elaborate word-play: so weighed down with depression that although I try to think about nothing, even that nothing—'no thought'—makes me feel tired and frightened.

33 *conceit*: imagination, fancifulness.

34 *Conceit*: thinking.
still: always.

36 *nothing . . . grief*: nothing has caused my grief about something.

37 *something . . . grieve*: something has caused me to grieve about nothing.

38 *'Tis in reversion . . . possess*: it is coming to me, I'm going to inherit it.

39–40 *what . . . name*: I can't give a name to something when I don't yet know what it is.

40 *wot*: know, suffer.

42 *shipp'd*: set sail.

46 *retir'd*: withdrawn.

48 *strongly*: with a strong army.

49 *repeals*: recalls from exile.

50 *with uplifted arms*: up in arms (*or perhaps* with arms uplifted in thanksgiving).

52 *that*: what.

57 *revolted faction*: rebellious dissidents.

59 *staff*: staff of office; Worcester was Steward of the royal Household.

60 *Household servants*: These included noblemen and all staff holding office at court (the 'ten thousand men' of which Richard boasts at *4, 1, 281–2*).

63 *heir*: offspring—i.e. the newly-born object of the queen's grief.

64 *prodigy*: monstrous birth.

65–6 *a gasping . . . join'd*: The queen sees herself as a mother for whom the pain of childbirth is increased by the grief of knowing she has borne a monster.

69 *cozening*: cheating, deceitful.

71 *Who*: i.e. death.
   bands: bonds.

72 *lingers in extremity*: prolongs to the utmost limit.

74 *with signs . . . neck*: i.e. wearing his gorget (= an iron collar worn by civilians to indicate military status).
   aged: agèd.

75 *careful business*: anxiety and preoccupation.

76 *comfortable words*: words of comfort.

79 *crosses*: frustrations, burdens.

80 *to save . . . off*: i.e. to keep Ireland under the government of the English crown.

82 *underprop*: support, take the weight of.

85 *try*: put to the test.

86 *your son . . . came*: Evidently York had been hoping for assistance in governing the kingdom—but Aumerle (as we find in *Act 3, Scene 2*) is with Richard in Ireland.

Green
We have, whereupon the Earl of Worcester
Hath broke his staff, resign'd his stewardship,
60 And all the Household servants fled with him
To Bullingbrook.
Queen
So, Green, thou art the midwife to my woe
And Bullingbrook my sorrow's dismal heir.
Now hath my soul brought forth her prodigy
65 And I, a gasping new-deliver'd mother,
Have woe to woe, sorrow to sorrow join'd.
Bushy
Despair not, madam.
Queen
                                    Who shall hinder me?
I will despair, and be at enmity
With cozening hope. He is a flatterer,
70 A parasite, a keeper-back of death
Who gently would dissolve the bands of life
Which false hope lingers in extremity.

Enter York

Green
Here comes the Duke of York.
Queen
With signs of war about his aged neck.
75 Oh, full of careful business are his looks!
Uncle, for God's sake speak comfortable words.
York
Should I do so I should belie my thoughts.
Comfort's in heaven and we are on the earth
Where nothing lives but crosses, cares, and grief.
80 Your husband, he is gone to save far off
Whilst others come to make him lose at home.
Here am I left to underprop his land
Who weak with age cannot support myself.
Now comes the sick hour that his surfeit made,
85 Now shall he try his friends that flatter'd him.

Enter a Servingman

Servingman
My lord, your son was gone before I came.

88   *cold*: unsympathetic.

90   *Sirrah*: A form of address used only to inferiors.
     sister: sister-in-law.
91   *presently*: immediately.
92   *take my ring*: i.e. to prove that he comes from York.
94   *called*: callèd.

98   *God . . . mercy*: may God have mercy. York may be praying for the soul of the duchess—or for God to assist him in this time of need.
101 *So my untruth*: provided my disloyalty.
102 *cut my head off . . . brother's*: York remembers the death of Gloucester.
103 *What*: York calls for attendants.
     posts: messengers.
105 *sister . . . cousin*: York is distracted, mistaking the queen for his dead sister-in-law.
106 *home*: i.e. to the royal Household.

112 *oath*: oath of allegiance to the monarch.

115 *kindred*: kinship, relationship.
117 *dispose of*: make some arrangements for. York now remembers that the Household is dispersed and so the queen needs accommodation.
118 *Berkeley Castle*: The castle, near the town of Berkeley, is on the banks of the Severn.
119 *should to*: ought to go to.
121 *at six and seven*: in total disorder; the proverbial expression comes from dicing.

York
He was? Why so, go all which way it will.
The nobles they are fled, the commons cold,
And will, I fear, revolt on Herford's side.
90 Sirrah, get thee to Plashy, to my sister Gloucester.
Bid her send me presently a thousand pound.
Hold, take my ring.
    Servingman
My lord, I had forgot to tell your lordship.
Today as I came by I called there—
95 But I shall grieve you to report the rest.
    York
What is't, knave?
    Servingman
An hour before I came the duchess died.
    York
God for His mercy! What a tide of woes
Comes rushing on this woeful land at once!
100 I know not what to do. I would to God,
So my untruth had not provok'd him to it,
The king had cut off my head with my brother's.
What, are there no posts despatch'd for Ireland?
How shall we do for money for these wars?
105 Come, sister—cousin I would say, pray pardon me.
Go, fellow, get thee home. Provide some carts
And bring away the armour that is there.
                    [*Exit* Servingman
Gentlemen, will you go muster men?
If I know how or which way to order these affairs
110 Thus disorderly thrust into my hands
Never believe me. Both are my kinsmen.
T'one is my sovereign, whom both my oath
And duty bids defend; t'other again
Is my kinsman, whom the king hath wrong'd,
115 Whom conscience and my kindred bids to right.
Well, somewhat we must do. Come, cousin.
I'll dispose of you. Gentlemen, go muster up your men
And meet me presently at Berkeley Castle.
I should to Plashy too,
120 But time will not permit. All is uneven
And everything is left at six and seven.
                    [*Exeunt* York *and* Queen

122 *sits fair*: is settled in a good direction.

126 *those love*: those who love.

130 *Wherein*: in which matter.
generally condemn'd: condemned by
everybody.
131 *judgement lie in them*: they are to be the
judges.
132 *ever*: always.

133 *Bristow*: An early form of Bristol.
134 *The Earl of Wiltshire*: Although the
character has twice been mentioned
(2, 1, 215 and 256), he has not appeared
on stage.
135 *office*: service, kindness.
136 *hateful*: full of hatred.

140 *heart's presages*: what my heart foretells.
not vain: not meaningless—i.e. have any
meaning.

144 *numbering . . . dry*: These are both
proverbially impossible tasks.

Bushy
The wind sits fair for news to go for Ireland
But none returns. For us to levy power
Proportionable to the enemy is all unpossible.
Green
125 Besides, our nearness to the king in love
Is near the hate of those love not the king.
Bagot
And that's the wavering commons, for their love
Lies in their purses, and whoso empties them
By so much fills their hearts with deadly hate.
Bushy
130 Wherein the king stands generally condemn'd.
Bagot
If judgement lie in them then so do we,
Because we ever have been near the king.
Green
Well, I will for refuge straight to Bristow Castle.
The Earl of Wiltshire is already there.
Bushy
135 Thither will I with you, for little office
Will the hateful commons perform for us,
Except like curs to tear us all to pieces.
Will you go along with us?
Bagot
No, I will to Ireland to his majesty.
140 Farewell. If heart's presages be not vain
We three here part that ne'er shall meet again.
Bushy
That's as York thrives to beat back Bullingbrook.
Green
Alas, poor duke! The task he undertakes
Is numbering sands and drinking oceans dry.
145 Where one on his side fights thousands will fly.
Farewell at once, for once, for all, and ever.
Bushy
Well, we may meet again.
Bagot
                                    I fear me never.   [*Exeunt*

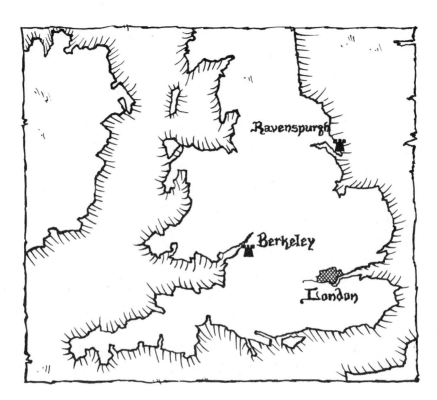

Act 2   Scene 3

Bullingbrook, travelling south with
Northumberland, is joined by Harry Percy
and others sympathetic to his cause. Outside
Berkeley Castle they are challenged by York,
who reproves Bullingbrook for his apparent
rebellion. Bullingbrook states his case,
assuring York that he has come only to claim
his rights. The location of the scene shifts
from Gloucestershire to Berkeley.

5 *Draws out*: lengthens.
6 *fair discourse*: Northumberland attempts
   to flatter Bullingbrook—who speaks
   very little!
7 *delectable*: The word is stressed on first
   and third syllables.
9 *Cotshall*: the Cotswolds.
10 *In*: by.
   wanting: being without.
11 *protest*: declare.
   beguil'd: diverted, amused.
12 *tediousness and process*: tedious process.

Scene 3

Gloucestershire. Enter Bullingbrook *and*
Northumberland

Bullingbrook
How far is it, my lord, to Berkeley now?
Northumberland
Believe me, noble lord,
I am a stranger here in Gloucestershire.
These high wild hills and rough uneven ways
5 Draws out our miles and makes them wearisome.
And yet your fair discourse hath been as sugar,
Making the hard way sweet and delectable.
But I bethink me what a weary way
From Ravenspurgh to Cotshall will be found
10 In Ross and Willoughby, wanting your company,
Which I protest hath very much beguil'd
The tediousness and process of my travel.
But theirs is sweeten'd with the hope to have

15 *in joy*: enjoyable.
16 *By this*: with this hope.

The present benefit which I possess,

15 And hope to joy is little less in joy

Than hope enjoy'd. By this the weary lords

Shall make their way seem short as mine hath done

By sight of what I have, your noble company.

Bullingbrook

Of much less value is my company

20 Than your good words. But who comes here?

Enter Harry Percy

Northumberland

It is my son, young Harry Percy,

Sent from my brother Worcester whencesoever.

Harry, how fares your uncle?

Percy

I had thought, my lord, to have learn'd his health of
you.

Northumberland

25 Why, is he not with the queen?

Percy

No, my good lord, he hath forsook the court,

Broken his staff of office and dispers'd

The Household of the king.

Northumberland

What was his reason?

He was not so resolv'd when last we spake together.

Percy

30 Because your lordship was proclaimed traitor.

But he, my lord, is gone to Ravenspurgh

To offer service to the Duke of Herford,

And sent me over by Berkeley to discover

What power the Duke of York had levied there,

35 Then with directions to repair to Ravenspurgh.

Northumberland

Have you forgot the Duke of Herford, boy?

Percy

No, my good lord, for that is not forgot

Which ne'er I did remember. To my knowledge

I never in my life did look on him.

Northumberland

40 Then learn to know him now. This is the duke.

21 *Harry Percy*: The historical character,
    better known as 'Hotspur', was in fact
    two years older than Bullingbrook.
22 *whencesoever*: from wherever he may be.

26–8 Harry Percy reports the same news
      that Green had brought to the queen in
      2, 2, 58–61.

30 *proclaimed*: proclaimèd.

35 *repair*: make my way.

36 *boy*: Northumberland rebukes his son.

Percy

My gracious lord, I tender you my service,
Such as it is, being tender, raw, and young,
Which elder days shall ripen and confirm
To more approved service and desert.

Bullingbrook

45 I thank thee, gentle Percy, and be sure
I count myself in nothing else so happy
As in a soul remembering my good friends,
And as my fortune ripens with thy love
It shall be still thy true love's recompense.
50 My heart this covenant makes, my hand thus seals it.

Northumberland

How far is it to Berkeley, and what stir
Keeps good old York there with his men of war?

Percy

There stands the castle by yon tuft of trees,
Mann'd with three hundred men as I have heard,
55 And in it are the lords of York, Berkeley, and
       Seymour,
None else of name and noble estimate.

Enter Ross *and* Willoughby

Northumberland

Here come the lords of Ross and Willoughby,
Bloody with spurring, fiery red with haste.

Bullingbrook

Welcome, my lords. I wot your love pursues
60 A banish'd traitor. All my treasury
Is yet but unfelt thanks, which, more enrich'd,
Shall be your love and labour's recompense.

Ross

Your presence makes us rich, most noble lord.

Willoughby

And far surmounts our labour to attain it.

Bullingbrook

65 Evermore thank's the exchequer of the poor,
Which till my infant fortune comes to years
Stands for my bounty. But who comes here?

Enter Berkeley

---

41 *tender*: submissively offer.

42 *tender, raw*: inexperienced, untrained.

44 *approved . . . desert*: service tested and found worthy.
    approved: approvèd.

45 *gentle*: noble.

47 *soul remembering*: heart that remembers.

48 *fortune*: good luck *and* wealth.

49 *still*: always.
    recompense: reward.

50 *thus*: Bullingbrook confirms the bargain by shaking hands.

51 *stir*: business, trouble.

55 *Berkeley*: i.e. the lord of the castle.

56 *estimate*: rank.

58 *Bloody*: i.e. the horses' sides are bloody.

59 *wot*: assume, believe.

60-2 *All . . . recompense*: Bullingbrook elaborates on his promise to Harry Percy.

61 *unfelt*: intangible, i.e. verbal, in words only.

65 *Evermore . . . exchequer*: 'thank you' is always—or always will be—the currency.

66 *comes to years*: matures.

67 *Stands*: represents.

Northumberland
It is my lord of Berkeley, as I guess.
    Berkeley
My lord of Herford, my message is to you.
    Bullingbrook
70 My lord, my answer is, to Lancaster,
    And I am come to seek that name in England,
    And I must find that title in your tongue
    Before I make reply to aught you say.
    Berkeley
    Mistake me not, my lord, 'tis not my meaning
75 To raze one title of your honour out.
    To you, my lord, I come—what lord you will—
    From the most gracious regent of this land,
    The Duke of York, to know what pricks you on
    To take advantage of the absent time
80 And fright our native peace with self-born arms?

       Enter York

    Bullingbrook
    I shall not need transport my words by you.
    Here comes his grace in person. My noble uncle.
      [*Kneels*]
    York
    Show me thy humble heart and not thy knee,
    Whose duty is deceivable and false.
    Bullingbrook
85 My gracious uncle—
    York
    Tut, tut! Grace me no grace, nor uncle me no uncle.
    I am no traitor's uncle, and that word grace
    In an ungracious mouth is but profane.
    Why have those banish'd and forbidden legs
90 Dar'd once to touch a dust of England's ground?
    But then, more why? Why have they dar'd to march
    So many miles upon her peaceful bosom,
    Frighting her pale-fac'd villages with war
    And ostentation of despised arms?
95 Comest thou because the anointed king is hence?
    Why, foolish boy, the king is left behind
    And in my loyal bosom lies his power.
    Were I but now lord of such hot youth

---

70 *my answer . . . Lancaster*: I answer only to the name of Lancaster (although Bullingbrook had accepted 'Herford' from Northumberland at line 36).

75 *raze*: omit, erase.
one title: Berkeley mocks Bullingbrook's dignity with a pun on 'tittle' (= smallest part).

79 *the absent time*: the time when the king is absent.
80 *self-born arms*: weapons carried in your own and not the country's cause.

84 *duty*: i.e. the act of kneeling.

86 *Grace . . . uncle*: York is impatient of his nephew's courtesy.
87 *that word grace*: The word is rich with spiritual overtones.
88 *profane*: blasphemous.
90 *a dust of*: a speck of dust on.
91 *But then, more why*: but even if that can be answered there are more questions.

94 *ostentation*: display, demonstration.
despised: despisèd; contemptible (because 'self-born').
96 *the king . . . behind*: Although Richard is in Ireland, the king's power has been deputed to York.

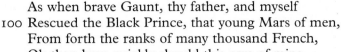

99–101 There is no obvious source for this claim.

100 *the Black Prince*: i.e. King Richard's father.

103 *palsy*: shaking sickness.
chastise: The stress is on first syllable.

106 *On what . . . wherein*: what law have I broken.

111 *braving arms*: flaunting defiance.

112 *I . . . Herford*: when I was banished I was only the Duke of Hereford.

113 *for*: Bullingbrook returns as the Duke of Lancaster *and* to claim the title of Lancaster.

115 *indifferent*: impartial.

118–19 *condemn'd A*: condemned as a.

119 *rights and royalties*: rights granted by the monarch and prerogatives of royal blood: Bullingbrook echoes the words of York's own protest to the king in 2, 1, 190.

120 *perforce*: forcibly.

121 *unthrifts*: wastrels, prodigals.

122–3 *If that . . . Lancaster*: Bullingbrook again echoes the words that York had used when he pleaded with Richard on his nephew's behalf in 2, 1, 191–9.

127 *rouse . . . bay*: Bullingbrook uses a metaphor from stag-hunting (= to start the quarry and hunt it to the point of surrender).

128–9 *sue . . . leave*: Bullingbrook again echoes the words of York at 2, 1, 202–4.

128 *denied*: refused the right.

As when brave Gaunt, thy father, and myself
100 Rescued the Black Prince, that young Mars of men,
From forth the ranks of many thousand French,
Oh then how quickly should this arm of mine,
Now prisoner to the palsy, chastise thee
And minister correction to thy fault!

Bullingbrook
105 My gracious uncle, let me know my fault.
On what condition stands it and wherein?

York
Even in condition of the worst degree,
In gross rebellion and detested treason.
Thou art a banish'd man, and here art come
110 Before the expiration of thy time
In braving arms against thy sovereign.

Bullingbrook
As I was banish'd, I was banish'd Herford;
But as I come, I come for Lancaster.
And, noble uncle, I beseech your grace
115 Look on my wrongs with an indifferent eye.
You are my father, for methinks in you
I see old Gaunt alive. Oh then, my father,
Will you permit that I shall stand condemn'd
A wandering vagabond, my rights and royalties
120 Pluck'd from my arms perforce and given away
To upstart unthrifts? Wherefore was I born?
If that my cousin king be king in England
It must be granted I am Duke of Lancaster.
You have a son, Aumerle, my noble cousin.
125 Had you first died and he been thus trod down
He should have found his uncle Gaunt a father
To rouse his wrongs and chase them to the bay.
I am denied to sue my livery here,

129 *letters patents*: official permit (open letter from the sovereign).	And yet my letters patents give me leave.
130 *distrain'd*: seized by law.	130 My father's goods are all distrain'd and sold,
	And these and all are all amiss employ'd.
	What would you have me do? I am a subject,
133 *challenge law*: demand my legal rights.	And I challenge law. Attorneys are denied me,
	And therefore personally I lay my claim
135 *of free descent*: through legal descent.	135 To my inheritance of free descent.

Northumberland
The noble duke hath been too much abus'd.

Ross
It stands your grace upon to do him right.

137 *stands . . . upon*: is incumbent on you.

Willoughby
Base men by his endowments are made great.

138 *his endowments*: the states with which Bullingbrook had been endowed.

York
My lords of England, let me tell you this:

140 *had feeling*: been aware.

140 I have had feeling of my cousin's wrongs
And labour'd all I could to do him right.

142 *kind*: manner.

But in this kind to come, in braving arms,

143 *his own carver*: help himself to what he wants.

Be his own carver and cut out his way,

144 *to find . . . wrong*: use improper means to achieve his rights.

To find out right with wrong? It may not be.

145 *abet*: aid, assist.

145 And you that do abet him in this kind
Cherish rebellion and are rebels all.

Northumberland
The noble duke hath sworn his coming is
But for his own, and for the right of that

148 *But*: only.

We all have strongly sworn to give him aid.

150 And let him ne'er see joy that breaks that oath.

York
Well, well. I see the issue of these arms.

151 *issue*: outcome.

I cannot mend it, I must needs confess,

153 *all ill-left*: everything has been left in poor condition.

Because my power is weak and all ill-left.
But if I could, by Him that gave me life

155 *attach*: arrest.
stoop: kneel to beg forgiveness.

155 I would attach you all and make you stoop
Unto the sovereign mercy of the king.
But since I cannot, be it known unto you
I do remain as neuter. So fare you well,
Unless you please to enter in the castle

160 And there repose you for this night.

162 *win*: persuade; Bullingbrook knows that York is weakening.

Bullingbrook
An offer, uncle, that we will accept.

164 *Bushy, Bagot*: Shakespeare has forgotten that, at 2, 2, 139, Bagot decided to join Richard in Ireland while *Green* went to Bristol with Bushy.
complices: accomplices.

But we must win your grace to go with us
To Bristow Castle, which they say is held
By Bushy, Bagot, and their complices,

165 *caterpillars of the commonwealth*: parasites on society; the expression (also used in *Woodstock*) is not unusual for the time.

166 *weed . . . away*: i.e. 'weed' the commonwealth and pluck away the 'caterpillars'.

169 *Nor . . . nor*: neither . . . nor.

165 The caterpillars of the commonwealth,
Which I have sworn to weed and pluck away.
York
It may be I will go with you, but yet I'll pause,
For I am loath to break our country's laws.
Nor friends nor foes to me welcome you are.
170 Things past redress are now with me past care.

[*Exeunt*

Act 2 | Scene 4

Richard has still not returned from Ireland and the Welsh soldiers, fearing the worst, have disbanded and deserted him. The omens are bad!

1 *stay'd*: waited.
2 *hardly*: with difficulty.
3 *yet*: still, so far.

8 *bay trees . . . wither'd*: A bad omen: a crown of bay leaves, symbolic of victory and immortal reputation, was the Roman reward for military triumph.
9 *meteors*: shooting stars.
   fixed stars: fixèd; Ptolemaic astronomy distinguished between the 'moving stars' (i.e. the planets) and 'fixed stars', which were attached to the firmament.
10 *looks bloody*: This could refer to influence as well as appearance.
11 *lean look'd*: hungry looking, lean faced.
   prophets: soothsayers, astrologers.
13 *enjoy*: possess.

Scene 4

Wales. Enter Earl of Salisbury *and a Welsh* Captain

Captain
My lord of Salisbury, we have stay'd ten days
And hardly kept our countrymen together,
And yet we hear no tidings from the king.
Therefore we will disperse ourselves. Farewell.

Salisbury
5 Stay yet another day, thou trusty Welshman.
The king reposeth all his confidence in thee.

Captain
'Tis thought the king is dead. We will not stay.
The bay trees in our country are all wither'd
And meteors fright the fixed stars of heaven.
10 The pale fac'd moon looks bloody on the earth,
And lean look'd prophets whisper fearful change.
Rich men look sad and ruffians dance and leap,
The one in fear to lose what they enjoy,
The other to enjoy by rage and war.

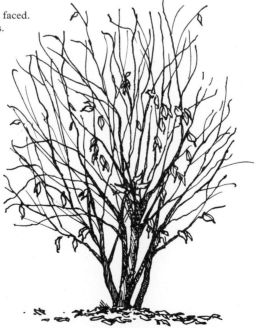

15 These signs forerun the death or fall of kings.
Farewell. Our countrymen are gone and fled
As well assur'd Richard their king is dead.   [*Exit*
       Salisbury
Ah, Richard! With the eyes of heavy mind
I see thy glory like a shooting star
20 Fall to the base earth from the firmament.
Thy sun sets weeping in the lowly west,
Witnessing storms to come, woe and unrest.
Thy friends are fled to wait upon thy foes
And crossly to thy good all fortune goes.   [*Exit*

22 *Witnessing*: forecasting, betokening.

24 *crossly*: adversely.

Act 3

Bullingbrook, disclaiming any personal motive for his action, denounces Bushy and Green and sentences them to death.

3 *presently*: immediately.
  part: leave.
4 *urging*: emphasizing, convincing you of.
5-6 *wash . . . hands*: clear myself of personal responsibility. To show that the executions are legally justified, Bullingbrook imitates the action of Pontius Pilate at the trial of Jesus: 'he took water, and washed his hands before the multitude, saying "I am innocent of the blood of this just person"' (Matthew 27:24).
7 *causes of*: legal reasons for.
9 *happy . . . lineaments*: gentleman fortunate in birth and personal appearance.
10 *clean*: utterly.
11-12 *You . . . and him*: This accusation does not appear to be borne out by the relations between Richard and his queen in the rest of the play; see 'Authentic?', p. xxv.
11 *in manner*: in a way, as it were.
12 *divorce*: breach, separation.
13 *Broke . . . bed*: Holinshed hints at adultery, fornication, and possibly homosexuality in his accusations of the king.
  possession: joint rights.
20 *in foreign clouds*: in obscurity under foreign skies.
22 *my signories*: estates, properties of which I am lord.
23 *Dispark'd my parks*: converted my hunting preserves to other (less aristocratic) uses.
24 *household coat*: the Bullingbrook coat-of-arms (which were displayed in the stained-glass windows).

Scene 1

Bristol. Enter Bullingbrook, York, Northumberland, Ross, Percy, Willoughby, *with* Bushy *and* Green *prisoners*

Bullingbrook
Bring forth these men.
Bushy and Green, I will not vex your souls,
Since presently your souls must part your bodies,
With too much urging your pernicious lives,
5 For 'twere no charity. Yet to wash your blood
From off my hands, here in the view of men
I will unfold some causes of your deaths.
You have misled a prince, a royal king,
A happy gentleman in blood and lineaments
10 By you unhappied and disfigur'd clean.
You have in manner with your sinful hours
Made a divorce betwixt his queen and him,
Broke the possession of a royal bed
And stain'd the beauty of a fair queen's cheeks
15 With tears drawn from her eyes by your foul wrongs.
Myself, a prince by fortune of my birth,
Near to the king in blood and near in love
Till you did make him misinterpret me,
Have stoop'd my neck under your injuries
20 And sigh'd my English breath in foreign clouds,
Eating the bitter bread of banishment
Whilst you have fed upon my signories,
Dispark'd my parks and fell'd my forest woods,
From my own windows torn my household coat,

25 *Raz'd*: scratched.
   imprese: personal emblem, painted on wood and incorporating a version of the household coat-of-arms, which was carried in tournaments and similar events.
27 *gentleman*: nobleman.

36 *at your house*: York had promised (2, 2, 117) to find accommodation for the queen when the royal Household was dispersed.
37 *intreated*: treated.
38 *commends*: regards.

41 *at large*: in full.
43 *To fight . . . complices*: This line could well be a late insertion: without it lines 42 and 44 end the scene neatly with a rhymed couplet. Glendower is not mentioned anywhere else in this play, but he is an important character in *Henry IV Part 1*, the next play in the tetralogy.

Act 3   Scene 2

Richard arrives in Wales just as Bullingbrook has announced his intention (at the end of Scene 1) to fight Glendower and the Welsh rebels. The king's joy at homecoming is quickly dispelled by reports of Bullingbrook's progress, the execution of the men who were his favourites and councillors, and the defection of all his own followers.

os.d. *colours*: banners.
 1 *Barkloughly*: Harlech; the version derives from Holinshed ('Barclowlie'). *at hand*: close by.
 2 *brooks*: enjoys.
 3 *late*: recent. *breaking*: rough.
 4 *Needs must I*: I am forced to.

25 Raz'd out my imprese, leaving me no sign
   Save men's opinions and my living blood
   To show the world I am a gentleman.
   This and much more, much more than twice all this,
   Condemns you to the death. See them deliver'd over
30 To execution and the hand of death.
        Bushy
   More welcome is the stroke of death to me
   Than Bullingbrook to England. Lords, farewell.
        Green
   My comfort is that heaven will take our souls
   And plague injustice with the pains of hell.
        Bullingbrook
35 My Lord Northumberland, see them dispatch'd.
            [*Exeunt* Northumberland *and* prisoners
   Uncle, you say the queen is at your house.
   For God's sake fairly let her be intreated.
   Tell her I send to her my kind commends.
   Take special care my greetings be deliver'd.
        York
40 A gentleman of mine I have dispatch'd
   With letters of your love to her at large.
        Bullingbrook
   Thanks, gentle uncle. Come, lords, away,
   To fight with Glendower and his complices.
   A while to work, and after holiday.   [*Exeunt*

Scene 2

> *Wales. Drums, flourish and colours. Enter*
> Richard, Aumerle, Carlisle, *and* soldiers

        Richard
Barkloughly Castle call they this at hand?
        Aumerle
Yea, my lord. How brooks your grace the air
After your late tossing on the breaking seas?
        Richard
Needs must I like it well. I weep for joy

6 *salute*: greet; Richard bends to touch the ground.

8 *long-parted*: having been long separated.

9 *fondly*: affectionately *and also* foolishly.

13 *sweets*: fruits.
ravenous sense: devouring appetite.

14 *spiders . . . venom*: The Elizabethans believed that spiders were venomous, and that they sucked up their poison from the ground.

15 *heavy-gaited*: lumbering.
toads: These were also believed to be poisonous.

17 *usurping*: i.e. usurping the ground which the toad should inhabit; perhaps anticipating Bullingbrook's intention.

21 *double*: forked.
mortal: deadly.

23 *senseless conjuration*: invocation to that which is without feeling.

24 *have a feeling*: become conscious.

24–5 *stones . . . soldiers*: Soldiers sprang from the earth when Cadmus (in classical mythology) sowed dragon's teeth.

25 *armed*: armèd.
native: natural; Richard in fact was born in Bordeaux.

27 *Fear not*: have no doubt.

29–32 *The means . . . redress*: i.e. we must accept and not refuse whatever heaven can offer, otherwise we shall deny the will of heaven. These lines were omitted from the Folio text, perhaps on grounds of obscurity—although the next comment from Aumerle makes it clear that the other characters are rather baffled by the bishop's words.

33 *remiss*: neglectful.

34 *security*: complacency, overconfidence.

35 *substance*: wealth.
power: forces.

36 *Discomfortable*: depressing, disheartening.

37 *eye of heaven*: i.e. the sun, 'king' of the planets.

5 To stand upon my kingdom once again.
Dear earth, I do salute thee with my hand,
Though rebels wound thee with their horses' hooves.
As a long-parted mother with her child
Plays fondly with her tears and smiles in meeting,
10 So weeping, smiling, greet I thee, my earth,
And do thee favours with my royal hands.
Feed not thy sovereign's foe, my gentle earth,
Nor with thy sweets comfort his ravenous sense
But let thy spiders that suck up thy venom
15 And heavy-gaited toads lie in their way,
Doing annoyance to the treacherous feet
Which with usurping steps do trample thee.
Yield stinging nettles to mine enemies,
And when they from thy bosom pluck a flower
20 Guard it, I pray thee, with a lurking adder
Whose double tongue may with a mortal touch
Throw death upon thy sovereign's enemies.
Mock not my senseless conjuration, lords.
This earth shall have a feeling and these stones
25 Prove armed soldiers ere her native king
Shall falter under foul rebellion's arms.

Carlisle
Fear not, my lord. That power that made you king
Hath power to keep you king in spite of all.
The means that heavens yield must be embrac'd
30 And not neglected. Else heaven would
And we will not. Heavens offer, we refuse
The proffer'd means of succour and redress.

Aumerle
He means, my lord, that we are too remiss
Whilst Bullingbrook through our security
35 Grows strong and great in substance and in power.

Richard
Discomfortable cousin, knowest thou not
That when the searching eye of heaven is hid
Behind the globe and lights the lower world
Then thieves and robbers range abroad unseen
40 In murders and in outrage boldly here.
But when from under this terrestrial ball
He fires the proud tops of the eastern pines
And darts his light through every guilty hole
Then murders, treasons, and detested sins,

38 *the lower world*: the antipodes.
41 *this terrestrial ball*: i.e. the 'globe' of
    line 38.
42 *fires*: lights up.
46 *at themselves*: at the revelation of their
    own wickedness.
49 *antipodes*: other side of the world—i.e.
    Ireland; Richard begins to develop his
    favourite image, the traditional
    comparison of the sun, the king of
    planets, and the monarch, king of men.
53 *self-affrighted*: frightened at the sight of
    themselves.
54 *rude*: stormy.
55 *balm*: consecrated oil.
56 *worldly men*: human beings.
57 *elected*: chosen.
58 *press'd*: impressed, conscripted.
59 *shrewd*: hurtful, injurious.

62 *still*: always.

64 *Nor near*: no nearer.

67 *One day*: arriving one day.

76 *But now*: just now.
    twenty thousand: Perhaps the
    discrepancy with line 70 arises from
    necessity of metre!
79 *pale and dead*: deathly pale.

45 The cloak of night being pluck'd from off their backs,
   Stand bare and naked, trembling at themselves?
   So when this thief, this traitor, Bullingbrook,
   Who all this while hath revell'd in the night
   Whilst we were wandering with the antipodes
50 Shall see us rising in our throne the east
   His treasons will sit blushing in his face,
   Not able to endure the sight of day,
   But self-affrighted tremble at his sin.
   Not all the water in the rough rude sea
55 Can wash the balm off from an anointed king.
   The breath of worldly men cannot depose
   The deputy elected by the Lord.
   For every man that Bullingbrook hath press'd
   To lift shrewd steel against our golden crown
60 God for His Richard hath in heavenly pay
   A glorious angel. Then if angels fight
   Weak men must fall, for heaven still guards the right.

                    Enter Salisbury

   Welcome, my lord. How far off lies your power?
           Salisbury
   Nor near nor farther off, my gracious lord,
65 Than this weak arm. Discomfort guides my tongue
   And bids me speak of nothing but despair.
   One day too late, I fear me, noble lord,
   Hath clouded all thy happy days on earth.
   Oh call back yesterday, bid time return
70 And thou shalt have twelve thousand fighting men.
   Today, today, unhappy day too late
   O'erthrows thy joys, friends, fortune, and thy state,
   For all the Welshmen, hearing thou wert dead,
   Are gone to Bullingbrook, dispers'd and fled.
           Aumerle
75 Comfort, my liege. Why looks your grace so pale?
           Richard
   But now the blood of twenty thousand men
   Did triumph in my face, and they are fled,
   And till so much blood thither come again
   Have I not reason to look pale and dead?
80 All souls that will be safe fly from my side,
   For time hath set a blot upon my pride.

Aumerle

Comfort, my liege. Remember who you are.

Richard

I had forgot myself. Am I not king?
Awake, thou coward! Majesty, thou sleepest.
85 Is not the king's name twenty thousand names?
Arm, arm, my name! A puny subject strikes
At thy great glory. Look not to the ground.
Ye favourites of a king, are we not high?
High be our thoughts. I know my uncle York
90 Hath power enough to serve our turn. But who
    comes here?

Enter Scroope

Scroope

More health and happiness betide my liege
Than can my care-tun'd tongue deliver him.

Richard

My ear is open and my heart prepar'd.
The worst is worldly loss thou canst unfold.
95 Say, is my kingdom lost? Why, 'twas my care
And what loss is it to be rid of care?
Strives Bullingbrook to be as great as we,
Greater he shall not be. If he serve God
We'll serve Him too, and be his fellow so.
100 Revolt our subjects? That we cannot mend.
They break their faith to God as well as us.
Cry woe, destruction, ruin and decay.
The worst is death, and death will have his day.

Scroope

Glad am I that your highness is so arm'd
105 To bear the tidings of calamity.
Like an unseasonable stormy day
Which makes the silver rivers drown their shores
As if the world were all dissolv'd to tears,
So high above his limits swells the rage
110 Of Bullingbrook, covering your fearful land
With hard bright steel and hearts harder than steel.
Whitebeards have arm'd their thin and hairless scalps
Against thy majesty, boys with women's voices
Strive to speak big, and clap their female joints
115 In stiff unwieldy arms against thy crown.
Thy very beadsmen learn to bend their bows

90 *serve our turn*: for our needs.

92 *care-tun'd*: tuned by anxiety, tuned to
the note of sorrow.
deliver: bring to.

95 *care*: trouble.

99 *his fellow*: i.e. Bullingbrook's equal.

102 *Cry*: even if you proclaim.

104 *arm'd*: prepared.

109 *his limits*: its banks.
110 *fearful*: filled with fear.
111 *steel*: i.e. of arms and armour.
113 *women's voices*: unbroken voices.
114 *speak big*: talk like men.
clap: encase.
female: delicate, girlish.

116 *beadsmen*: pensioners (paid to say
prayers for their benefactors).

117 *double-fatal yew*: Yew was the wood,
     poisonous in itself, from which
     longbows were made.
118 *distaff women*: i.e. housewives; the distaff
     was used in spinning wool.
     manage: handle.
     rusty bills: bill-hooks rusty from disuse.
119 *seat*: throne, position.
122–3 *Where is . . . Green*: The audience
     knows what has happened to the Earl of
     Wiltshire, Bushy, and Green—but the
     whereabouts of Bagot are unknown.
125 *measure our confines*: travel over our
     territory.
129 *vipers . . . redemption*: The treachery of
     the viper was proverbial: 'Ye serpents,
     ye generation of vipers, how can ye
     escape the damnation of hell'
     (Matthew 23:33).
     without: beyond hope of.
131 *Snakes . . . heart*: Richard refers to the
     fable of the farmer who was fatally
     bitten by a snake which had been
     almost dead from cold until he warmed
     it inside his shirt.
132 *Three*: Richard apparently knows that
     Bagot is not with the other favourites.
     Judas: The disciple who betrayed Jesus:
     his name became a synonym for
     'traitor'.
134 *spotted*: stained, sinful.

Of double-fatal yew against thy state.
Yea, distaff women manage rusty bills
Against thy seat. Both young and old rebel
120 And all goes worse than I have power to tell.
    Richard
Too well, too well thou tell'st a tale so ill.
Where is the Earl of Wiltshire, where is Bagot,
What is become of Bushy, where is Green,
That they have let the dangerous enemy
125 Measure our confines with such peaceful steps?
If we prevail their heads shall pay for it.
I warrant they have made peace with Bullingbrook.
    Scroope
Peace have they made with him indeed, my lord.
    Richard
Oh villains, vipers, damn'd without redemption!
130 Dogs, easily won to fawn on any man!
Snakes in my heart blood warm'd, that sting my
   heart!
Three Judases, each one thrice worse than Judas!
Would they make peace? Terrible hell
Make war upon their spotted souls for this!

135 *his property*: its nature.

138 *not with hands*: i.e. not by signing treaties or shaking hands in friendship.

140 *grav'd*: buried
150 *deposed*: deposèd.
153–4 *small model . . . bones*: piece of earth that will cover our dead bodies, *and* body covering our bones.
154 *paste and cover*: piecrust, pastry covering.
155 *let us*: It is unlikely that any of the courtiers would sit down with Richard.
156 *sad*: unhappy, tragic.
158 *depos'd*: deprived of life.
162 *antic*: clown, jester: Death was frequently portrayed as a skeleton grinning at the futile pretensions of mankind.

163 *Scoffing*: ridiculing.
164 *a breath*: a breathing space, a short life.
   scene: The image of life as a play enacted on the stage of the world was common.
165 *monarchize*: play at being a king.
166 *self . . . conceit*: vain conceit of his own self-importance.
168 *humour'd thus*: [Death] being wilfully that way inclined, having amused himself like this.

Scroope
135 Sweet love I see, changing his property,
   Turns to the sourest and most deadly hate.
   Again uncurse their souls. Their peace is made
   With heads and not with hands. Those whom you curse
   Have felt the worst of death's destroying wound
140 And lie full low, grav'd in the hollow ground.
      Aumerle
   Is Bushy, Green, and the Earl of Wiltshire dead?
      Scroope
   Ay, all of them at Bristow lost their heads.
      Aumerle
   Where is the duke my father with his power?
      Richard
   No matter where. Of comfort no man speak.
145 Let's talk of graves, of worms and epitaphs,
   Make dust our paper and with rainy eyes
   Write sorrow on the bosom of the earth.
   Let's choose executors and talk of wills.
   And yet not so, for what can we bequeath
150 Save our deposed bodies to the ground?
   Our lands, our lives and all are Bullingbrook's,
   And nothing can we call our own but death,
   And that small model of the barren earth
   Which serves as paste and cover to our bones.
155 For God's sake let us sit upon the ground
   And tell sad stories of the death of kings,
   How some have been depos'd, some slain in war,
   Some haunted by the ghosts they have depos'd,
   Some poison'd by their wives, some sleeping kill'd,
160 All murder'd. For within the hollow crown
   That rounds the mortal temples of a king
   Keeps Death his court, and there the antic sits
   Scoffing his state and grinning at his pomp,
   Allowing him a breath, a little scene
165 To monarchize, be fear'd and kill with looks,
   Infusing him with self and vain conceit
   As if this flesh which walls about our life
   Were brass impregnable, and humour'd thus

169–70 *pin . . . wall*: The image changes and becomes that of an attack on a besieged castle.
171   *Cover*: Courtiers stood bareheaded in the presence of the monarch.

175   *want*: need.
176   *Subjected thus*: being made subject to all these.

179   *presently*: promptly.
       prevent: anticipate and consequently avoid.
       ways to wail: paths to grief.

183   *No worse . . . fight*: it can't be any worse [than being slain] if you fight.
184   *destroying*: defying.
185   *Where*: whereas.
       pays . . . breath: lives as a slave to death.
186   *power*: army.
       Enquire of him: enlist his help.
187   *make a body of a limb*: make a single troop as effective as an entire army.

189   *change*: exchange.
       our day of doom: the day that decides our fate.
190   *ague fit*: shivering attack; shivering and sweating alternate in the ague.
       overblown: passed away.

194   *complexion*: general appearance.

198   *torturer . . . and small*: Torture on the rack by stretching out the victim's limbs was made worse if the stretching were slow.

202   *gentlemen in arms*: gentlemen of rank (or *perhaps* gentlemen up in arms).
203   *party*: faction, side.

204   *Beshrew*: curse.
204–5 *forth Of*: away from.

Comes at the last and with a little pin
170 Bores through his castle wall and farewell king!
Cover your heads, and mock not flesh and blood
With solemn reverence. Throw away respect,
Tradition, form, and ceremonious duty,
For you have but mistook me all this while.
175 I live with bread like you, feel want,
Taste grief, need friends. Subjected thus,
How can you say to me I am a king?
      Carlisle
My lord, wise men ne'er sit and wail their woes,
But presently prevent the ways to wail.
180 To fear the foe, since fear oppresseth strength,
Gives, in your weakness, strength unto your foe,
And so your follies fight against your self.
Fear and be slain. No worse can come to fight,
And fight and die is death destroying death
185 Where fearing dying pays death servile breath.
      Aumerle
My father hath a power. Enquire of him
And learn to make a body of a limb.
      Richard
Thou chid'st me well. Proud Bullingbrook, I come
To change blows with thee for our day of doom.
190 This ague fit of fear is overblown,
An easy task it is to win our own.
Say, Scroope, where lies our uncle with his power?
Speak sweetly, man, although thy looks be sour.
      Scroope
Men judge by the complexion of the sky
195 The state and inclination of the day;
So may you by my dull and heavy eye.
My tongue hath but a heavier tale to say.
I play the torturer by small and small
To lengthen out the worst that must be spoken.
200 Your uncle York is join'd with Bullingbrook
And all your northern castles yielded up,
And all your southern gentlemen in arms
Upon his party.
      Richard
              Thou hast said enough.
[*To* Aumerle] Beshrew thee, cousin, which didst
  lead me forth

205 Of that sweet way I was in to despair.
    What say you now? What comfort have we now?
    By heaven I'll hate him everlastingly
    That bids me be of comfort any more.
    Go to Flint Castle, there I'll pine away.
210 A king, woe's slave, shall kingly woe obey.
    That power I have, discharge, and let them go
    To ear the land that hath some hope to grow,
    For I have none. Let no man speak again
    To alter this, for counsel is but vain.
         Aumerle
215 My liege, one word.
         Richard
                        He does me double wrong
    That wounds me with the flatteries of his tongue.
    Discharge my followers, let them hence away
    From Richard's night to Bullingbrook's fair day.
                        [*Exeunt*

209 *Flint*: A town in the north of Wales near Chester.

212 *ear*: cultivate.
    the land: i.e. (metaphorically) Bullingbrook and his cause.

215 *double wrong*: What Richard sees as the flattery of 'My liege' wounds as much as the offer of false hope.

218 *Richard's night . . . day*: Richard surrenders his 'sun-king' image to Bullingbrook.

Act 3   Scene 3

Bullingbrook and his supporters reach Flint
Castle and Bullingbrook, speaking through
Northumberland, demands restitution of his
rights. Richard appears on the balcony and
laments his misfortunes, then descends to
the main stage and, unresisting, yields
himself into Bullingbrook's hands.

os.d. *colours*: banners.
1 *intelligence*: military information;
   Bullingbrook enters in the middle of a
   conversation.

Scene 3

Flint Castle. Enter with drum and colours
Bullingbrook, York, Northumberland,
Attendants

Bullingbrook
So that by this intelligence we learn
The Welshmen are dispers'd, and Salisbury
Is gone to meet the king, who lately landed
With some few private friends upon this coast.

Northumberland

5 The news is very fair and good, my lord.
Richard not far from hence hath hid his head.

York

It would beseem the Lord Northumberland
To say King Richard. Alack the heavy day
When such a sacred king should hide his head.

Northumberland

10 Your grace mistakes. Only to be brief
Left I his title out.

York

                              The time hath been,
Would you have been so brief with him he would
Have been so brief with you to shorten you,
For taking so the head, your whole head's length.

Bullingbrook

15 Mistake not, uncle, further than you should.

York

Take not, good cousin, further than you should,
Lest you mistake. The heavens are o'er our heads.

Bullingbrook

I know it, uncle, and oppose not myself
Against their will. But who comes here?

Enter Percy

20 Welcome, Harry. What, will not this castle yield?

Percy

The castle royally is mann'd, my lord,
Against thy entrance.

Bullingbrook

Royally? Why, it contains no king.

Percy

Yes, my good lord.

25 It doth contain a king. King Richard lies
Within the limits of yon lime and stone,
And with him are the Lord Aumerle, Lord Salisbury,
Sir Stephen Scroope, besides a clergyman
Of holy reverence; who, I cannot learn.

Northumberland

30 Oh, belike it is the Bishop of Carlisle.

Bullingbrook

Noble lord,
Go to the rude ribs of that ancient castle.

---

6 *hid his head*: taken shelter;
Northumberland is contemptuous.

7 *beseem*: become, be appropriate for.

13 *to*: as to.

14 *taking . . . head*: speaking in this way to
the head of state and being so
headstrong as to omit his title.

15 *Mistake not*: don't (deliberately)
misunderstand.

17 *lest . . . mistake*: for fear you take what is
not yours.
The heavens . . . heads: i.e. God is
watching over us.

20 *this castle*: i.e. Flint Castle.

25 *lies*: resides, dwells.

31 *Noble lord*: i.e. probably
Northumberland.

32 *rude ribs*: rough walls.

33 *breath of parle*: call of invitation to conference.
34 *his ruin'd ears*: i.e. the hearing of the castle.
35 *Henry Bullingbrook*: The half-line asserts the name's importance.

40 *my . . . repeal'd*: my sentence of banishment may be revoked.
42 *advantage of my power*: superiority of my forces.
43 *summer*: The month was August, 1399.
45–8 Bullingbrook's attitude changes from insolence to humility—perhaps in response to a reproving glance from his uncle.

48 *stooping*: kneeling in submission. *tenderly*: respectfully.

52 *totter'd*: dilapidated, ruined.
53 *fair appointments*: impressive military showing.
55 *With*: causing.
56–7 *shock . . . heaven*: Bullingbrook alludes to the belief that thunder was caused by a clash between the opposing elements of fire and water in the form of lightning and rain.

62s.d *Parle without . . . walls*: The trumpets on stage ('*without*') sound the call and a response is given by the trumpets backstage ('*within*'); then a fanfare heralds the appearance of the king on the balcony at the back of the stage.
63 *blushing discontented sun*: A red sunrise usually presages a stormy day.
65 *he*: i.e. the sun. *envious*: hostile.

69 *eagle*: The eagle was king among birds.
69–70 *lightens . . . majesty*: gives out royal glances like lightning.

Through brazen trumpet send the breath of parle
Into his ruin'd ears, and thus deliver:
35 Henry Bullingbrook
On both his knees doth kiss King Richard's hand
And sends allegiance and true faith of heart
To his most royal person; hither come
Even at his feet to lay my arms and power,
40 Provided that my banishment repeal'd
And lands restor'd again be freely granted.
If not I'll use the advantage of my power
And lay the summer's dust with showers of blood
Rain'd from the wounds of slaughter'd Englishmen,
45 The which how far off from the mind of
        Bullingbrook
It is such crimson tempest should bedrench
The fresh green lap of fair King Richard's land
My stooping duty tenderly shall show.
Go, signify as much while here we march
50 Upon the grassy carpet of this plain.
Let's march without the noise of threatening drum,
That from this castle's totter'd battlements
Our fair appointments may be well perus'd.
Methinks King Richard and myself should meet
55 With no less terror than the elements
Of fire and water when their thundering shock
At meeting tears the cloudy cheeks of heaven.
Be he the fire, I'll be the yielding water.
The rage be his, whilst on the earth I rain
60 My waters; on the earth and not on him.
March on, and mark King Richard how he looks.

Parle without, and answer within. Then a
flourish. Enter on the walls Richard,
Carlisle, Aumerle, Scroope, Salisbury

See, see, King Richard doth himself appear
As doth the blushing discontented sun
From out the fiery portal of the east
65 When he perceives the envious clouds are bent
To dim his glory and to stain the track
Of his bright passage to the occident.
York
Yet looks he like a king. Behold, his eye,
As bright as is the eagle's, lightens forth

71 *show*: appearance.	

70 Controlling majesty. Alack, alack for woe
That any harm should stain so fair a show.
   Richard
[*To* Northumberland] We are amaz'd, and thus long
   have we stood
To watch the fearful bending of thy knee
Because we thought ourself thy lawful king.
75 And if we be, how dare thy joints forget
To pay their awful duty to our presence?
If we be not, show us the hand of God
That hath dismiss'd us from our stewardship,
For well we know no hand of blood and bone
80 Can gripe the sacred handle of our sceptre,
Unless he do profane, steal, or usurp.
And though you think that all as you have done
Have torn their souls by turning them from us
And we are barren and bereft of friends
85 Yet know: my master, God omnipotent,
Is mustering in his clouds on our behalf
Armies of pestilence, and they shall strike
Your children yet unborn and unbegot
That lift your vassal hands against my head
90 And threat the glory of my precious crown.
Tell Bullingbrook, for yon methinks he stands,
That every stride he makes upon my land
Is dangerous treason. He is come to ope
The purple testament of bleeding war,
95 But ere the crown he looks for live in peace
Ten thousand bloody crowns of mothers' sons
Shall ill become the flower of England's face,
Change the complexion of her maid-pale peace
To scarlet indignation and bedew
100 Her pastor's grass with faithful English blood.
   Northumberland
The King of Heaven forbid our lord the king
Should so with civil and uncivil arms
Be rush'd upon! Thy thrice noble cousin,
Harry Bullingbrook, doth humbly kiss thy hand
105 And by the honourable tomb he swears,
That stands upon your royal grandsire's bones,
And by the royalties of both your bloods,
Currents that spring from one most gracious head,
And by the buried hand of warlike Gaunt,

72 *amaz'd*: puzzled, bewildered.

73 *To watch*: in expectation of seeing.
   fearful: showing fear.

76 *awful duty*: dutiful reverence.
77 *hand*: authority, handwriting.

80 *gripe*: grasp.
81 *profane*: commit an act of sacrilege.

83 *torn*: jeopardized.

87 *pestilence*: plague.

89 *vassal*: subject, servile.

91 *yon*: yonder, over there.

93–4 *to ope . . . war*: to start a bloody war
   which will leave a legacy of bloodshed.
95 *looks for*: is hoping for.
96 *crowns*: heads.

100 *pastor's grass*: Richard visualizes the king
   as shepherd of his subjects.

102 *civil . . . arms*: brutal weapons in civil
   war.
103 *thrice noble*: Bullingbrook's 'nobility' (as
   Northumberland details in the next
   lines) derives from Edward III, from
   John of Gaunt, and from his own
   deserts.
105 *honourable tomb*: i.e. that of Edward III
   in Westminster Abbey.
107 *royalties*: royal status, regality.

113 *lineal royalties*: hereditary rights of royalty.
114 *Enfranchisement*: restoration of legitimate authorities.
115 *thy royal party*: your majesty's side of the agreement.
granted once: i.e. once this has been granted.
116 *commend*: hand over.
117 *barbed*: barbèd; armed (with spikes on their heads).

120 *credit*: believe.
121 *returns*: sends back the answer.
126 *Speak . . . commends*: Northumberland withdraws silently and without ceremony.
128 *look so poorly*: seem so abject.
fair: courteously.

136 *sooth*: appeasement.

140 *Swell'st thou*: do you beat faster, do you swell with pride.
141 *scope*: aim, purpose.
beat: (a) punish; (b) defeat; (c) whip.

110 And by the worth and honour of himself,
Comprising all that may be sworn or said,
His coming hither hath no further scope
Than for his lineal royalties, and to beg
Enfranchisement immediate on his knees,
115 Which on thy royal party granted once
His glittering arms he will commend to rust,
His barbed steeds to stables and his heart
To faithful service of your majesty.
This swears he as he is a prince and just,
120 And as I am a gentleman I credit him.
        Richard
Northumberland, say thus the king returns:
His noble cousin is right welcome hither,
And all the number of his fair demands
Shall be accomplish'd without contradiction.
125 With all the gracious utterance thou hast
Speak to his gentle hearing kind commends.
[*To* Aumerle] We do debase ourselves, cousin, do
        we not,
To look so poorly and to speak so fair?
Shall we call back Northumberland and send
130 Defiance to the traitor and so die?
        Aumerle
No, good my lord. Let's fight with gentle words,
Till time lend friends, and friends their helpful
        swords.
        Richard
Oh God, oh God, that e'er this tongue of mine
That laid the sentence of dread banishment
135 On yon proud man should take it off again
With words of sooth! Oh that I were as great
As is my grief, or lesser than my name,
Or that I could forget what I have been,
Or not remember what I must be now!
140 Swell'st thou, proud heart? I'll give thee scope to
        beat,
Since foes have scope to beat both thee and me.

        Aumerle
Northumberland comes back from Bullingbrook.
        Richard
What must the king do now? Must he submit?
The king shall do it. Must he be depos'd?

145 The king shall be contented. Must he lose
The name of king? A God's name let it go.
I'll give my jewels for a set of beads,
My gorgeous palace for a hermitage,
My gay apparel for an almsman's gown,

150 My figur'd goblets for a dish of wood,
My sceptre for a palmer's walking staff,
My subjects for a pair of carved saints,
And my large kingdom for a little grave,
A little, little grave, an obscure grave,

155 Or I'll be buried in the king's highway,
Some way of common trade, where subjects' feet
May hourly trample on their sovereign's head;
For on my heart they tread now whilst I live,
And buried once, why not upon my head?

160 Aumerle, thou weep'st, my tender-hearted cousin.
We'll make foul weather with despised tears:
Our sighs and they shall lodge the summer corn
And make a dearth in this revolting land.
Or shall we play the wantons with our woes

165 And make some pretty match with shedding tears,
As thus to drop them still upon one place
Till they have fretted us a pair of graves
Within the earth, and therein laid? There lies
Two kinsmen digg'd their graves with weeping eyes.

170 Would not this ill do well? Well, well, I see
I talk but idly and you laugh at me.
Most mighty prince, my Lord Northumberland.
What says King Bullingbrook? Will his majesty
Give Richard leave to live till Richard die?

175 You make a leg and Bullingbrook says ay.

---

145 *contented*: in agreement.

147–54 Richard solemnly abjures the world
    to prepare for his spiritual pilgrimage
    towards death.
147 *set of beads*: a rosary.
149 *almsman*: recipient of charity.
150 *figur'd*: embossed, decorated.
151 *palmer*: pilgrim bound for Jerusalem.
152 *carved*: carvèd.

156 *trade*: traffic (with a pun on 'tread' in
    line 158).

159 *buried once*: once I am buried.

161 *despised tears*: despisèd; (a) tears of
    those who are despised; (b) tears which
    we have formerly despised.
162 *Our sighs and they*: i.e. like wind and
    rain.
    lodge: flatten, beat down.
163 *revolting*: rebellious.
164 *play the wantons*: amuse ourselves.
165 *pretty match*: clever game.
166 *still*: continually.
167 *fretted us*: worn away for us.
168–9 *There . . . eyes*: i.e. as epitaph on the
    graves.
170 *ill*: (a) wickedness; (b) unhappiness.
171 *idly*: foolishly.
172 *Most mighty prince*: Richard's heavy
    irony announces the return of
    Northumberland.
175 *make a leg*: bend your knee.

176 *base court*: i.e. the servants' courtyard.

Northumberland
My lord, in the base court he doth attend
To speak with you. May it please you to come down?
    Richard
Down, down I come, like glistering Phaëton,
Wanting the manage of unruly jades.

178–9 *Phaëton . . . jades*: Phaëton (the name
    is pronounced with three syllables) stole
    the chariot of his father, the sun-god
    Phoebus Apollo; unable to control
    ('manage') the headstrong horses, he
    drove too close to the earth—which was
    only saved from destruction when Jove
    killed him with a thunderbolt.
180–2 *Base court . . . base court*: Richard
    plays with the different senses of 'base'
    (= corrupt, menial, low-down) and
    'court' (= royal court, courtyard).
181 *do them grace*: (a) behave graciously to
    them; (b) bow to them.
183 *night owls*: The owl was associated with
    darkness, evil, and death.

180 In the base court? Base court where kings grow base
To come at traitors' calls and do them grace!
In the base court come down. Down court, down
    king,
For night owls shriek where mounting larks should
    sing.

Richard descends

    Bullingbrook
What says his majesty?
    Northumberland
                        Sorrow and grief of heart
185 Makes him speak fondly like a frantic man.

184–5 *What says . . . man*: The two lines
    allow time for Richard to descend
    (offstage) from the balcony and enter
    through the main stage doors.
185 *fondly*: foolishly.
    frantic man: madman.

Enter Richard *below*

Yet he is come.
    Bullingbrook
                    Stand all apart
And show fair duty to his majesty.

186 *Stand all apart*: Bullingbrook instructs
    his men to stand at a respectful distance
    from Richard.
187 *fair duty*: proper respect (by kneeling).

He kneels down

My gracious lord.
    Richard
Fair cousin, you debase your princely knee

189–90 *debase . . . base earth*: Richard
    continues to play on the word 'base'.
191 *Me rather had*: I would rather, I would
    prefer that.
192 *courtesy*: kneeling (curtsy), obeisance.

190 To make the base earth proud with kissing it.
Me rather had my heart might feel your love
Than my unpleas'd eye see your courtesy.

Up, cousin, up. Your heart is up, I know,
Thus high at least, although your knee be low.

Bullingbrook

195 My gracious lord, I come but for mine own.

Richard

Your own is yours and I am yours and all.

Bullingbrook

So far be mine, my most redoubted lord,
As my true service shall deserve your love.

Richard

Well you deserve. They well deserve to have
200 That know the strong'st and surest way to get.
Uncle, give me your hands. Nay, dry your eyes.
Tears show their love but want their remedies.
Cousin, I am too young to be your father,
Though you are old enough to be my heir.
205 What you will have I'll give, and willing too,
For do we must what force will have us do.
Set on towards London, cousin, is it so?

Bullingbrook

Yea, my good lord.

Richard

                    Then I must not say no.

Flourish   [*Exeunt*

Act 3   Scene 4

The queen overhears the gardeners, who are
discussing the state of the nation.

194 *Thus high at least*: Richard indicates the
crown on his head.

197 *redoubted*: dreaded.

202 *their love*: i.e. the love of those who shed
the tears.
want their remedies: cannot cure the
misfortunes they lament.

1 *this garden*: The queen's words indicate
the location of this scene.

3 *bowls*: Bowling greens were often found
in Elizabethan gardens—and the game
provided many metaphors!
4 *rubs*: hindrances to the run of the
bowls, difficulties.

Scene 4

A garden. Enter the Queen *with her*
Attendants

Queen

What sport shall we devise here in this garden
To drive away the heavy thought of care?

Lady

Madam, we'll play at bowls.

Queen

'Twill make me think the world is full of rubs

5 *bias*: weight inserted into side of bowl to make it run a particular way.

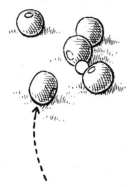

7 *measure*: (a) musical time; (b) a stately dance.
8 *no measure keeps*: is limitless.
13 *wanting*: lacking.
14 *remember*: remind.
15 *being altogether had*: since I have so much of it.

18 *boots not*: is pointless.
complain: lament.

22 *I could . . . good*: if weeping could do any good, I would now be singing (having already wept so much).

25 *these trees*: i.e. the stage posts; the queen's words direct the audience's imagination.
26 *My wretchedness*: I will wager my wretchedness.
unto: against.
row of pins: i.e. something very trivial.
28 *Against*: in anticipation of.
forerun: heralded.

5 And that my fortune runs against the bias.
    Lady
Madam, we'll dance.
    Queen
My legs can keep no measure in delight
When my poor heart no measure keeps in grief.
Therefore no dancing, girl. Some other sport.
    Lady
10 Madam, we'll tell tales.
    Queen
Of sorrow or of joy?
    Lady
                Of either, madam.
    Queen
Of neither, girl.
For if of joy, being altogether wanting
It doth remember me the more of sorrow,
15 Or if of grief, being altogether had
It adds more sorrow to my want of joy.
For what I have I need not to repeat
And what I want it boots not to complain.
    Lady
Madam, I'll sing.
    Queen
            'Tis well that thou hast cause,
20 But thou shouldst please me better wouldst thou weep.
    Lady
I could weep, madam, would it do you good.
    Queen
And I could sing would weeping do me good,
And never borrow any tear of thee.

Enter a Gardener *and two* Servants

But stay, here come the gardeners.
25 Let's step into the shadow of these trees.
My wretchedness unto a row of pins
They'll talk of state, for everyone doth so
Against a change. Woe is forerun with woe.

Gardener

Go bind thou up young dangling apricocks,
30 Which like unruly children make their sire
Stoop with oppression of their prodigal weight.
Give some supportance to the bending twigs.
Go thou, and like an executioner
Cut off the heads of too-fast-growing sprays
35 That look too lofty in our commonwealth.
All must be even in our government.
You thus employ'd, I will go root away
The noisome weeds which without profit suck
The soil's fertility from wholesome flowers.

Servant

40 Why should we, in the compass of a pale,
Keep law and form and due proportion,
Showing as in a model our firm estate,
When our sea-walled garden, the whole land,
Is full of weeds, her fairest flowers chok'd up,
45 Her fruit trees all unprun'd, her hedges ruin'd,
Her knots disorder'd and her wholesome herbs
Swarming with caterpillars?

29 *apricocks*: An early form of 'apricots'.

31 *prodigal*: wasteful, extravagant.

35 *lofty*: tall and overbearing.

38 *noisome*: foul.

40 *pale*: fenced enclosure.

42 *in a model*: in miniature.
43 *walled*: wallèd.

46 *knots*: formal flowerbeds in intricate designs.

Gardener

Hold thy peace.

He that hath suffer'd this disorder'd spring

Hath now himself met with the fall of leaf.

50 The weeds which his broad spreading leaves did shelter,

That seem'd in eating him to hold him up,

Are pluck'd up root and all by Bullingbrook.

I mean the Earl of Wiltshire, Bushy, Green.

Servant

What, are they dead?

Gardener

They are, and Bullingbrook

55 Hath seiz'd the wasteful king. Oh what pity is it

That he had not so trimm'd and dress'd his land

As we this garden! We at time of year

Do wound the bark, the skin of our fruit trees,

Lest being overproud in sap and blood

60 With too much riches it confound itself.

Had he done so to great and growing men

They might have liv'd to bear and he to taste

Their fruits of duty. Superfluous branches

We lop away, that bearing boughs may live.

65 Had he done so, himself had borne the crown

Which waste of idle hours hath quite thrown down.

Servant

What, think you then the king shall be depos'd?

Gardener

Depress'd he is already, and depos'd

'Tis doubt he will be. Letters came last night

70 To a dear friend of the good Duke of York's

That tell black tidings.

Queen

Oh, I am press'd to death through want of speaking!

Thou, old Adam's likeness set to dress this garden,

How dares thy harsh rude tongue sound this unpleasing news?

75 What Eve, what serpent hath suggested thee

To make a second fall of cursed man?

Why dost thou say King Richard is depos'd?

Darest thou, thou little better thing than earth,

Divine his downfall? Say where, when, and how

---

48 *suffer'd*: (a) permitted; (b) experienced.

49 *fall of leaf*: i.e. autumn.

51 *seem'd . . . up*: i.e. they were parasites, like ivy.

57 *at time of year*: in the proper season.

59 *overproud*: excessively swollen.

60 *confound*: ruin.

64 *bearing*: fruit-bearing.

68 *Depress'd*: brought lower.

69 *'Tis doubt*: it is feared.

72 *press'd to death*: Pressing to death was the punishment for defendants who refused to speak at their trials. *press'd*: oppressed, worried.

73 *Adam*: Adam was said to be the archetypal gardener because he was put into the Garden of Eden 'to dress it and to keep it' (Genesis 2:15). *dress*: tend.

75–6 *Eve . . . man*: The first 'fall of man' happened when Adam and Eve (who was tempted by the devil in the likeness of a snake) disobeyed God's commandment and were expelled from the Garden of Eden (Genesis chapter 3).

75 *suggested*: tempted.

76 *cursed*: cursèd.

79 *Divine*: predict.

80 Camest thou by this ill tidings? Speak, thou wretch!
   Gardener
Pardon me, madam. Little joy have I
To breathe this news, yet what I say is true.
King Richard he is in the mighty hold
Of Bullingbrook. Their fortunes both are weigh'd.

83 *hold*: power, wrestling hold.
84 *weigh'd*: balanced against each other.

85 In your lord's scale is nothing but himself
And some few vanities that make him light,
But in the balance of great Bullingbrook
Besides himself are all the English peers,
And with that odds he weighs King Richard down.
90 Post you to London and you'll find it so.
I speak no more than everyone doth know.

86 *vanities*: follies, fools (i.e. the favourites, who are balanced against 'all the English peers' in line 88).

89 *odds*: advantage, superiority.

90 *Post*: hasten.

Queen

Nimble mischance, that art so light of foot,
Doth not thy embassage belong to me,
And am I last that knows it? Oh, thou thinkest
95 To serve me last that I may longest keep
Thy sorrow in my breast. Come ladies, go
To meet at London London's king in woe.
What, was I born to this, that my sad look
Should grace the triumph of great Bullingbrook?
100 Gardener, for telling me these news of woe
Pray God the plants thou graft'st may never grow.
                           [*Exit with* Attendants

Gardener

Poor queen, so that thy state might be no worse
I would my skill were subject to thy curse.
Here did she fall a tear. Here in this place
105 I'll set a bank of rue, sour herb of grace.
Rue even for ruth here shortly shall be seen
In the remembrance of a weeping queen.
                           [*Exeunt*

93 *embassage*: ambassadorial message.
   belong to: concern.

95 *serve*: e.g. with food at a meal, or with a
   legal document.

96–101 The rhymes show the queen
   regaining control of herself and the
   situation.

99 *grace the triumph*: adorn the triumphal
   procession.

102 *so that*: if only.

104 *fall*: let fall.

105 *rue . . . grace*: The herb rue was known
   as 'herb of grace' because it was
   associated with repentance, which
   comes by the grace of God.

106 *for ruth*: out of pity, as a symbol of pity.

Act 4

Act 4   Scene 1

Bullingbrook hears the dispute between
Bagot and Aumerle and their supporters but
adjourns the hearing. He sends for
Richard—although Carlisle protests. Richard
conducts his own ceremony of deposition,
but refuses to read the Articles. He is
arrested and sent to prison. Westminster
discloses a plot to Carlisle and Aumerle.

os.d. *as to the Parliament*: The scene calls
    for a throne-room, and the royal regalia
    would be carried at the head of the
    procession.
2 *freely speak*: Bullingbrook echoes the
    words spoken by Richard in the first
    scene (*1, 1, 17*).
4 *wrought . . . king*: talked the king into it.
5 *office*: deed.
    timeless: untimely.

9 *unsay*: deny.
    deliver'd: spoken.
10 *dead*: (a) fatal; (b) secret.

13 *Calais*: i.e. where Gloucester was killed.
14 *that very time*: on the same occasion.
    This in fact would have been
    impossible: Bullingbrook had not then
    been exiled.
16 *an . . . crowns*: i.e. about £25,000.
17 *Than Bullingbrook's return*: than that
    Bullingbrook should return.
18 *withal*: as well.

Scene 1

Westminster Hall. Enter as to the Parliament
Bullingbrook, Aumerle, Northumberland,
Percy, Fitzwater, Surrey, the Bishop of
Carlisle, the Abbot of Westminster,
Herald, Officers, *and* Bagot

Bullingbrook
Call forth Bagot.
Now, Bagot, freely speak thy mind
What thou dost know of noble Gloucester's death,
Who wrought it with the king, and who perform'd
5 The bloody office of his timeless end.
Bagot
Then set before my face the Lord Aumerle.
Bullingbrook
Cousin, stand forth, and look upon that man.
Bagot
My Lord Aumerle, I know your daring tongue
Scorns to unsay what once it hath deliver'd.
10 In that dead time when Gloucester's death was
    plotted
I heard you say 'Is not my arm of length,
That reacheth from the restful English court
As far as Calais, to mine uncle's head?'
Amongst much other talk that very time
15 I heard you say that you had rather refuse
The offer of an hundred thousand crowns
Than Bullingbrook's return to England,
Adding withal how bless'd this land would be
In this your cousin's death.

Aumerle

Princes and noble lords,

20 What answer shall I make to this base man?
Shall I so much dishonour my fair stars
On equal terms to give him chastisement?
Either I must, or have mine honour soil'd
With the attainder of his slanderous lips.

25 There is my gage, the manual seal of death
That marks thee out for hell. I say thou liest,
And will maintain what thou hast said is false
In thy heart blood, though being all too base
To stain the temper of my knightly sword.

Bullingbrook

30 Bagot, forbear. Thou shalt not take it up.

Aumerle

Excepting one, I would he were the best
In all this presence that hath mov'd me so.

Fitzwater

If that thy valour stand on sympathy,
There is my gage, Aumerle, in gage to thine.

35 By that fair sun which shows me where thou standest
I heard thee say, and vauntingly thou spak'st it,
That thou wert cause of noble Gloucester's death.
If thou deniest it twenty times, thou liest,
And I will turn thy falsehood to thy heart

40 Where it was forged, with my rapier's point.

Aumerle

Thou dar'st not, coward, live to see that day.

Fitzwater

Now by my soul I would it were this hour.

Aumerle

Fitzwater, thou art damn'd to hell for this.

21 *dishonour . . . stars*: Aumerle, being of
higher rank, would degrade himself by
fighting Bagot.

24 *attainder*: dishonourable accusation,
slur.
25 *gage*: pawn, token thrown down in
challenge.
manual seal: as a seal from my hand—
i.e. like a signature or handshake.

29 *temper*: quality (of steel).

31 *excepting one*: i.e. except for
Bullingbrook.
the best: highest in rank.
32 *presence*: assembly, company.
mov'd: angered.
33 *stand on sympathy*: will only fight those
of your own rank.

34 *in gage*: engaged.
35 *that fair sun*: i.e. Bullingbrook.
36 *vauntingly*: boastfully.
40 *forged*: forgèd.
rapier: flexible, sharp-pointed sword
popular in Shakespeare's time: the
historical Fitzwater would have a flat-
bladed broadsword.

Percy
Aumerle, thou liest. His honour is as true

45 In this appeal as thou art all unjust,
And that thou art so, there I throw my gage,
To prove it on thee to the extremest point
Of mortal breathing. Seize it if thou darest.
Aumerle
And if I do not may my hands rot off

50 And never brandish more revengeful steel
Over the glittering helmet of my foe!
Another Lord
I task the earth to the like, forsworn Aumerle,
And spur thee on with full as many lies
As may be hollow'd in thy treacherous ear

55 From sun to sun. There is my honour's pawn.
Engage it to the trial if thou darest.
Aumerle
Who sets me else? By heaven, I'll throw at all!
I have a thousand spirits in one breast
To answer twenty thousand such as you.
Surrey

60 My Lord Fitzwater, I do remember well
The very time Aumerle and you did talk.
Fitzwater
'Tis very true, you were in presence then
And you can witness with me this is true.
Surrey
As false, by heaven, as heaven itself is true.
Fitzwater

65 Surrey, thou liest.
Surrey
                                Dishonourable boy,
That lie shall lie so heavy on my sword
That it shall render vengeance and revenge
Till thou the lie-giver and that lie do lie
In earth as quiet as thy father's skull.

70 In proof whereof there is my honour's pawn.
Engage it to the trial if thou darest.
Fitzwater
How fondly dost thou spur a forward horse!
If I dare eat or drink or breathe or live
I dare meet Surrey in a wilderness

45 *appeal*: accusation.
  all: entirely.

47–8 *to the extremest . . . breathing*: to the
  death.

50 *more*: again.

52–9 The Folio text of the play omits this
  lord and his 'gage' (although Holinshed
  records many more such gestures on
  this occasion).
52 *task*: burden—i.e. by throwing down yet
  another gage.
53 *full*: just, at least.
  lies: accusations of lying.
54 *hollow'd*: hollered, shouted.
55 *sun to sun*: sunrise to sunset (the formal
  limits for a duel).
57 *Who sets me else*: who else is betting:
  Aumerle speaks the language of
  gambling with dice.

62 *in presence*: present, in attendance on
  the king.
65 *boy*: An expression of contempt.
66 *That lie*: the accusation of lying and the
  lie itself; these lines are full of quibbles.
67 *it shall render*: my sword will give back
  in return.

72 *fondly*: foolishly.
  forward: willing, eager.

76 *There . . . faith*: Fitzwater points to his gauntlet (or else throws down a second gage).

77 *tie*: commit.

78 *this new world*: i.e. the world that Bullingbrook now rules.

79 *appeal*: accusation.

80 *banish'd Norfolk*: i.e. Mowbray.

83–4 *Some honest Christian . . . this*: Holinshed says that Aumerle borrowed a hood from a bystander.

85 *repeal'd*: recalled from his banishment. *try*: be tried for.

86 *rest under gage*: remain as challenges.

89 *signories*: estates.

93 *glorious Christian field*: i.e. as a crusader in the Holy Land.

94 *Streaming*: flying in the wind.

96 *retir'd himself*: withdrew.

103–4 *bosom . . . Abraham*: An expression of conventional piety: 'the beggar [Lazarus] died, and was carried by the angels into Abraham's bosom [= heaven]' (Luke 16:22).

104 *appellants*: accusers.

106 *we*: Bullingbrook is already adopting the royal plural.

108 *plume-pluck'd*: crestfallen, downcast.

75 And spit upon him whilst I say he lies
And lies and lies. There is my bond of faith
To tie thee to my strong correction.
As I intend to thrive in this new world
Aumerle is guilty of my true appeal.
80 Besides, I heard the banish'd Norfolk say
That thou, Aumerle, didst send two of thy men
To execute the noble duke at Calais.

Aumerle
Some honest Christian trust me with a gage.
That Norfolk lies, here do I throw down this,
85 If he may be repeal'd to try his honour.

Bullingbrook
These differences shall all rest under gage
Till Norfolk be repeal'd. Repeal'd he shall be
And, though mine enemy, restor'd again
To all his lands and signories. When he's return'd,
90 Against Aumerle we will enforce his trial.

Carlisle
That honourable day shall ne'er be seen.
Many a time hath banish'd Norfolk fought
For Jesu Christ in glorious Christian field,
Streaming the ensign of the Christian cross
95 Against black pagans, Turks, and Saracens,
And, toil'd with works of war, retir'd himself
To Italy, and there at Venice gave
His body to that pleasant country's earth
And his pure soul unto his captain, Christ,
100 Under whose colours he had fought so long.

Bullingbrook
Why, bishop, is Norfolk dead?

Carlisle
As surely as I live, my lord.

Bullingbrook
Sweet peace conduct his sweet soul to the bosom
Of good old Abraham. Lords appellants,
105 Your differences shall all rest under gage
Till we assign you to your days of trial.

Enter York

York
Great Duke of Lancaster, I come to thee
From plume-pluck'd Richard, who with willing soul

109 *Adopts thee heir*: York's statement
indicates that Richard has abdicated,
and is not therefore being deposed.

114 *Marry*: by [the Virgin] Mary.

115 *Worst*: most lowly; Carlisle recognizes
that he is only a priest among the
nobles.
this royal presence: Carlisle is sarcastic:
he proposes the correct form at line 117.

116 *best beseeming me*: I am the most
appropriate person.

117–49 Carlisle argues against the abdication
with a set speech in a classical form,
employing the rhetorical *genus humile*
(= lowly style) to protest against
Bullingbrook's high presumption.

119 *noblesse*: nobility (of soul as well as
rank), magnanimity.

120 *Learn him forbearance*: teach him to
refrain.

123 *but*: except when.
by: present.

124 *apparent*: evident, obvious.

125 *figure*: image.

126 *elect*: chosen.

127 *crowned*: crownèd.

128 *subject . . . breath*: the verdict of an
inferior subject.

129 *forfend*: forbid, prevent.

130 *souls refin'd*: civilized people.

134 *My lord of Herford*: The bishop uses the
title under which Bullingbrook was
exiled.

141 *kin with kin . . . confound*: cause
kinsmen and fellow-countrymen to
destroy each other.

144 *Golgotha*: The place where Jesus was
crucified whose name 'is, being
interpreted, the place of a skull'
(Mark 15:22).

145 *raise*: stir up to rebel.
this house . . . house: Carlisle refers to
the house of Parliament: 'And if a
house be divided against itself, that
house cannot stand' (Mark 3:25).

147 *cursed*: cursèd.

Adopts thee heir, and his high sceptre yields
110 To the possession of thy royal hand.
Ascend his throne, descending now from him,
And long live Henry, of that name the fourth!

Bullingbrook
In God's name I'll ascend the regal throne.

Carlisle
Marry, God forbid!
115 Worst in this royal presence may I speak,
Yet best beseeming me to speak the truth.
Would God that any in this noble presence
Were enough noble to be upright judge
Of noble Richard. Then true noblesse would
120 Learn him forbearance from so foul a wrong.
What subject can give sentence on his king,
And who sits here that is not Richard's subject?
Thieves are not judg'd but they are by to hear
Although apparent guilt be seen in them,
125 And shall the figure of God's majesty,
His captain, steward, deputy, elect,
Anointed, crowned, planted many years,
Be judg'd by subject and inferior breath
And he himself not present? Oh, forfend it, God,
130 That in a Christian climate souls refin'd
Should show so heinous, black, obscene a deed!
I speak to subjects and a subject speaks,
Stirr'd up by God thus boldly for his king.
My lord of Herford here, whom you call king,
135 Is a foul traitor to proud Herford's king,
And if you crown him let me prophesy:
The blood of English shall manure the ground
And future ages groan for this foul act.
Peace shall go sleep with Turks and infidels,
140 And in this seat of peace tumultuous wars
Shall kin with kin and kind with kind confound.
Disorder, horror, fear and mutiny
Shall here inhabit, and this land be call'd
The field of Golgotha and dead men's skulls.
145 Oh, if you raise this house against this house
It will the woefullest division prove
That ever fell upon this cursed earth.
Prevent it, resist it, let it not be so,
Lest child, child's children, cry against you woe.

151 *Of*: on a charge of.
154–317 These lines form the so-called 'deposition scene', and were omitted from the first three editions of the play; see 'Crisis in the Monarchy', p. iv.
154 *commons' suit*: This was a request for the publication of the terms of Richard's abdication.
155 *common*: public.
156 *surrender*: give up the crown, abdicate.

157 *conduct*: escort.

159 *sureties*: securities to ensure appearance. *answer*: trial.
160 *beholding*: indebted.
161 *look'd for*: expected.

162 *to a king*: Richard already thinks of himself as having surrendered the crown.
163 *shook*: shaken (a common Elizabethan form).
165 *insinuate*: slide myself forward.

168 *favours*: (a) faces; (b) political colours.

170 *So Judas did*: 'And forthwith he [Judas] came to Jesus and said "Hail, master", and kissed him' (Matthew 26:49). *twelve*: i.e. disciples, followers.

173 *both . . . clerk*: The clerk, or deacon, gave the response 'Amen' to the prayers spoken by the priest.
176 *service*: office, function.

178 *tired majesty*: tirèd; royalty in its formal dress.

Northumberland
150 Well have you argu'd, sir, and for your pains
     Of capital treason we arrest you here.
     My Lord of Westminster, be it your charge
     To keep him safely till his day of trial.
     May it please you, lords, to grant the commons' suit?
     Bullingbrook
155 Fetch hither Richard, that in common view
     He may surrender. So we shall proceed
     Without suspicion.
     York
                        I will be his conduct.   [*Exit*
     Bullingbrook
     Lords, you that here are under our arrest,
     Procure your sureties for your days of answer.
160 Little are we beholding to your love
     And little look'd for at your helping hands.

             Enter Richard *and* York

     Richard
     Alack, why am I sent for to a king
     Before I have shook off the regal thoughts
     Wherewith I reign'd? I hardly yet have learn'd
165 To insinuate, flatter, bow, and bend my knee.
     Give sorrow leave awhile to tutor me
     To this submission. Yet I well remember
     The favours of these men. Were they not mine?
     Did they not sometime cry 'All Hail' to me?
170 So Judas did to Christ, but he in twelve
     Found truth in all but one, I in twelve thousand
         none.
     God save the king! Will no man say Amen?
     Am I both priest and clerk? Well then, Amen.
     God save the king, although I be not he,
175 And yet Amen if heaven do think him me.
     To do what service am I sent for hither?
             York
     To do that office of thine own good will
     Which tired majesty did make thee offer,
     The resignation of thy state and crown
180 To Henry Bullingbrook.

Richard
Give me the crown. Here, cousin, seize the crown,
On this side my hand and on that side thine.
Now is this golden crown like a deep well
That owes two buckets, filling one another,
185 The emptier ever dancing in the air,
The other down, unseen and full of water.
That bucket, down and full of tears, am I,
Drinking my griefs whilst you mount up on high.
Bullingbrook
I thought you had been willing to resign.
Richard
190 My crown I am, but still my griefs are mine.
You may my glories and my state depose,
But not my griefs. Still am I king of those.
Bullingbrook
Part of your cares you give me with your crown.
Richard
Your cares set up do not pluck my cares down.
195 My care is loss of care, by old care done.
Your care is gain of care, by new care won.
The cares I give I have, though given away.
They 'tend the crown, yet still with me they stay.
Bullingbrook
Are you contented to resign the crown?
Richard
200 Aye—no. No—aye, for I must nothing be,
Therefore no 'no', for I resign to thee.
Now, mark me how I will undo myself.
I give this heavy weight from off my head
And this unwieldy sceptre from my hand,
205 The pride of kingly sway from out my heart.
With mine own tears I wash away my balm;
With mine own hands I give away my crown;
With mine own tongue deny my sacred state;
With mine own breath release all duteous oaths.

184 *owes*: owns, possesses.
  filling one another: i.e. when the full bucket is raised, the empty bucket is lowered to be filled in its turn.
185 *ever*: always.

194–8 *care*: Richard puns on several senses of this word: (a) obligation; (b) grief; (c) worry: 'the cause of my grief is my loss of responsibility, brought about by my former lack of diligence; the cause of your trouble is the access of responsibility achieved by your recent pains'.
198 *'tend*: are attendant upon.
200–1 *Aye—no . . . no 'no'*: Richard plays with the homophones 'I'/'aye', 'no'/'know'. The subtleties are expressed more clearly in Elizabethan texts, which spell 'I' for both 'I' and 'aye'.
200 *nothing*: no thing.
201 *no 'no', for I resign to thee*: i.e. I cannot say 'no', because in fact I *do* resign in your favour.
202 *undo*: (a) destroy; (b) undress. Richard divests himself of the emblems of majesty.
203 *heavy weight*: i.e. the crown.
206 *balm*: the holy oil of the coronation anointing.
209 *duteous oaths*: oaths of loyalty and duty.

211 *revenues*: The accent is on the second
    syllable.

214 *are made*: that are made.
215 *Make me*: May God make me.
    with nothing griev'd: grieved by nothing—
    and also, grieved by having nothing.

226 *deem*: judge.

227 *ravel out*: unravel, unweave.

231 *read . . . them*: read them aloud.
234 *oath*: i.e. Northumberland's oath of
    allegiance to Richard.
237 *bait*: torment.
238–41 *With Pilate . . . your sin*: The Roman
    Pontius Pilate washed his hands (as
    token that he was guiltless) before he
    delivered Jesus up to be crucified
    (Matthew 27:24). Bullingbrook has
    already invoked this parallel (*3, 1, 5–6*).

240 *deliver'd*: handed over; the same word is
    used in the Gospel accounts of the
    episode.
    sour: bitter.

210 All pomp and majesty I do forswear;
    My manors, rents, revenues I forgo;
    My acts, decrees, and statutes I deny.
    God pardon all oaths that are broke to me;
    God keep all vows unbroke are made to thee.
215 Make me that nothing have with nothing griev'd,
    And thou with all pleas'd that hast all achiev'd.
    Long mayst thou live in Richard's seat to sit,
    And soon lie Richard in an earthy pit.
    God save King Henry, unking'd Richard says,
220 And send him many years of sunshine days.
    What more remains?

Northumberland
                        No more, but that you read
    These accusations and these grievous crimes
    Committed by your person and your followers
    Against the state and profit of this land,
225 That by confessing them the souls of men
    May deem that you are worthily depos'd.

        Richard
    Must I do so? And must I ravel out
    My weav'd-up follies? Gentle Northumberland,
    If thy offences were upon record
230 Would it not shame thee, in so fair a troop,
    To read a lecture of them? If thou wouldst,
    There shouldst thou find one heinous Article
    Containing the deposing of a king
    And cracking the strong warrant of an oath,
235 Mark'd with a blot, damn'd in the book of heaven.
    Nay, all of you that stand and look upon me
    Whilst that my wretchedness doth bait my self,
    Though some of you with Pilate wash your hands,
    Showing an outward pity, yet you Pilates
240 Have here deliver'd me to my sour cross
    And water cannot wash away your sin.

242 *dispatch*: make haste.

245 *sort*: band, gang.

249 *pompous*: ceremonially dressed.

253 *haught*: arrogant, haughty.

255 *given . . . font*: with which I was
christened; certain followers of
Bullingbrook had asserted that Richard
was illegitimate.

256 *usurp'd*: taken away illegally. Richard
now attacks those who have taken away
his identity.

260 *sun of Bullingbrook*: The sun imagery is
now transferred from Richard to
Bullingbrook.

261 *water drops*: tears.

263 *And if*: if indeed.
sterling: valid currency.

266 *his*: its.

271 *commons*: They had requested (line 154)
that the terms of the abdication should
be published.

Northumberland
My lord, dispatch. Read o'er these Articles.
　　Richard
Mine eyes are full of tears; I cannot see.
And yet salt water blinds them not so much
245 But they can see a sort of traitors here.
Nay, if I turn mine eyes upon my self
I find myself a traitor with the rest,
For I have given here my soul's consent
T'undeck the pompous body of a king,
250 Made glory base, a sovereignty a slave,
Proud majesty a subject, state a peasant.
　　Northumberland
My lord—
　　Richard
No lord of thine, thou haught insulting man,
Nor no man's lord. I have no name, no title,
255 No, not that name was given me at the font,
But 'tis usurp'd. Alack the heavy day
That I have worn so many winters out
And know not now what name to call myself.
Oh that I were a mockery king of snow
260 Standing before the sun of Bullingbrook,
To melt myself away in water drops.
Good king, great king, and yet not greatly good,
And if my word be sterling yet in England
Let it command a mirror hither straight
265 That it may show me what a face I have
Since it is bankrupt of his majesty.
　　Bullingbrook
Go some of you, and fetch a looking glass.
　　　　　　　　　　[*Exit an* Attendant
　　Northumberland
Read o'er this paper while the glass doth come.
　　Richard
Fiend, thou torments me ere I come to hell.
　　Bullingbrook
270 Urge it no more, my Lord Northumberland.
　　Northumberland
The commons will not then be satisfied.

Richard
They shall be satisfied. I'll read enough
When I do see the very book indeed
Where all my sins are writ, and that's my self.

Enter one with a glass

275 Give me that glass and therein will I read.
No deeper wrinkles yet? Hath sorrow struck
So many blows upon this face of mine
And made no deeper wounds? Oh flattering glass,
Like to my followers in prosperity
280 Thou dost beguile me. Was this face the face
That every day under his household roof
Did keep ten thousand men? Was this the face
That like the sun did make beholders wink?
Is this the face which fac'd so many follies,
285 That was at last outfac'd by Bullingbrook?
A brittle glory shineth in this face.
As brittle as the glory is the face,

Smashes the glass

For there it is, crack'd in an hundred shivers.
Mark, silent king, the moral of this sport,
290 How soon my sorrow hath destroy'd my face.
Bullingbrook
The shadow of your sorrow hath destroy'd
The shadow of your face.

282 *ten thousand*: This number is vouched for by Holinshed.
283 *wink*: close their eyes.
284 *fac'd*: countenanced.
285 *outfac'd*: discountenanced, opposed.

288 *shivers*: fragments.

291-2 *shadow . . . your face*: the action provoked by your sorrow has destroyed the reflection of your face; Bullingbrook is contemptuous.

293 *shadow*: embodiment, expression.

296 *to*: compared to.

298 *There*: i.e. in the soul.
  substance: i.e. as opposed to shadow.

307 *to*: as.

314 *from your sights*: i.e. where I can't see any
  of you (and where you can't see me).
315 *convey him*: escort him.
316 *'convey'*: Richard develops the word to
  include its other senses of 'transfer the
  title of a property' and 'steal'.
317 *nimbly*: cleverly.
318–19 These two lines seem to originate
  with the censored stage version of the
  play (when the 'deposition' episode was
  cancelled) but they are printed,
  notwithstanding, in the Folio text on
  which this edition is based.
318 *set down*: appoint.

Richard
                              Say that again.
The shadow of my sorrow. Ha, let's see.
'Tis very true, my grief lies all within
295 And these external manners of laments
Are merely shadows to the unseen grief
That swells with silence in the tortur'd soul.
There lies the substance; and I thank thee, king,
For thy great bounty, that not only givest
300 Me cause to wail but teachest me the way
How to lament the cause. I'll beg one boon
And then be gone and trouble you no more.
Shall I obtain it?

Bullingbrook
                              Name it, fair cousin.

Richard
Fair cousin? I am greater than a king,
305 For when I was a king my flatterers
Were then but subjects. Being now a subject
I have a king here to my flatterer.
Being so great I have no need to beg.

Bullingbrook
Yet ask.

Richard
310 And shall I have?

Bullingbrook
You shall.

Richard
Then give me leave to go.

Bullingbrook
Whither?

Richard
Whither you will, so I were from your sights.

Bullingbrook
315 Go some of you, convey him to the Tower.

Richard
Oh good—'convey'. Conveyers are you all
That rise thus nimbly by a true king's fall.

Bullingbrook
On Wednesday next we solemnly set down
Our coronation. Lords, prepare yourselves.

[*Exeunt* Bullingbrook, Richard, Lords *and* guards,
all except Westminster, Carlisle, and Aumerle

Westminster

320 *pageant*: spectacle, performance.

320 A woeful pageant have we here beheld.

Carlisle

The woe's to come. The children yet unborn
Shall feel this day as sharp to them as thorn.

Aumerle

You holy clergymen, is there no plot
To rid the realm of this pernicious blot?

324 *blot*: stain (the shameful deed of deposing the monarch).

Westminster

325 My lord,
Before I freely speak my mind herein
You shall not only take the sacrament

327 *take the sacrament*: receive Holy Communion (thereby sealing their promise to keep faith).
328 *bury mine intents*: conceal my plans.

To bury mine intents but also to effect
Whatever I shall happen to devise.
330 I see your brows are full of discontent,
Your hearts of sorrow and your eyes of tears.
Come home with me to supper. I will lay
A plot shall show us all a merry day.

[*Exeunt*

Act 5

Act 5 Scene 1

Richard and his queen meet in a London
street and lament together. Northumberland
enters, separating them and ordering Richard
to go to Pomfret (Pontefract).

os.d. *Attendants*: These are presumably the
'Ladies' of *Act 3*, Scene 4.

2 *Julius Caesar's . . . tower*: It was
popularly believed that the Tower of
London had been built by Julius Caesar.
ill-erected: built with some evil intent, *or*,
built with evil result—i.e. that of
imprisoning Richard.

3 *flint*: flinty, merciless.
condemned: condemnèd.

8 *rose*: The rose was king among flowers—
as the lion was king among animals (see
line 34).

11 *model . . . stand*: little picture of ruined
Troy; the rather strained image arises
perhaps from 'Troynovant' (New Troy),
the name sometimes given to London.

12 *map*: image, outline.

13–15 *beauteous inn . . . guest*: The queen
portrays grief and triumph as temporary
residents, ugly ('hard-favoured') grief
being given the better accommodation.

18 *state*: stateliness, splendour.

20 *sworn brother*: member of a brotherhood
(either chivalric or monastic).

22 *keep a league*: maintain an alliance.
Hie thee: take yourself.

23 *cloister . . . house*: enter some nunnery.

24 *new world's crown*: i.e. a heavenly crown.

25 *Which . . . down*: which we have lost
through the wicked lives we have been
living here on earth; 'thrown' must be
pronounced with *two* syllables—
'thro-wen'.

Scene 1

A street in London. Enter the Queen *with
her* Attendants

Queen
This way the king will come. This is the way
To Julius Caesar's ill-erected tower,
To whose flint bosom my condemned lord
Is doom'd a prisoner by proud Bullingbrook.
5 Here let us rest, if this rebellious earth
Have any resting for her true king's queen.

Enter Richard *and* guard

But soft, but see, or rather do not see
My fair rose wither. Yet look up, behold,
That you in pity may dissolve to dew
10 And wash him fresh again with true love tears.
Ah thou, the model where old Troy did stand,
Thou map of honour, thou King Richard's tomb,
And not King Richard! Thou most beauteous inn,
Why should hard-favour'd grief be lodged in thee
15 When triumph is become an alehouse guest?
Richard
Join not with grief, fair woman, do not so,
To make my end too sudden. Learn, good soul,
To think our former state a happy dream,
From which awak'd, the truth of what we are
20 Shows us but this. I am sworn brother, sweet,
To grim Necessity, and he and I
Will keep a league till death. Hie thee to France
And cloister thee in some religious house.
Our holy lives must win a new world's crown
25 Which our profane hours here have thrown down.

26 *shape*: body, appearance.
27 *weakened*: weakenèd.

29–31 *The lion . . . o'erpower'd*: The image is
borrowed from Marlowe's *Edward II*:

> But when the imperial lion's flesh is
> gored
> He rents and tears it with his wrathful
> paw,
> And, highly scorning that the lowly
> earth,
> Should drink his blood, mounts up to
> the air.   (5, 1, 11–14)

31 *pupil-like*: like a schoolboy.
32 *kiss the rod*: willingly submit (a proverbial
expression).

35 *beasts indeed*: i.e. the powerful nobles
who have behaved like beasts.

37 *sometime*: former.

42 *betid*: happened (a rare past tense of
'betide').
43 *'quite their griefs*: requite, cap, their tales
of woe.

46 *For why*: yes indeed.
senseless: inanimate, unfeeling.
brands: firewood.
sympathize: respond to.
47 *moving*: evoking sympathy.
48 *weep the fire out*: i.e. by exuding resin.
49 *some*: i.e. some of the firebrands.
51 *Bullingbrook*: Northumberland still does
not use the title of 'king'.

52 *Pomfret*: Pontefract Castle in Yorkshire.
53 *there . . . ta'en*: arrangements have been
made.
54 *France*: Richard's queen was French,
and is being returned to her family.

Queen
What, is my Richard both in shape and mind
Transform'd and weakened? Hath Bullingbrook
Depos'd thine intellect? Hath he been in thy heart?
The lion dying thrusteth forth his paw
30 And wounds the earth if nothing else with rage
To be o'erpower'd, and wilt thou, pupil-like,
Take the correction mildly, kiss the rod,
And fawn on rage with base humility,
Which art a lion and the king of beasts?

Richard
35 A king of beasts indeed. If aught but beasts
I had been still a happy king of men.
Good sometime queen, prepare thee hence for
    France.
Think I am dead, and that even here thou takest
As from my deathbed thy last living leave.
40 In winter's tedious nights sit by the fire
With good old folks, and let them tell thee tales
Of woeful ages, long ago betid,
And ere thou bid good night, to 'quite their griefs
Tell thou the lamentable tale of me
45 And send the hearers weeping to their beds.
For why! the senseless brands will sympathize
The heavy accent of thy moving tongue,
And in compassion weep the fire out,
And some will mourn in ashes, some coal black,
50 For the deposing of a rightful king.

Enter Northumberland

Northumberland
My lord, the mind of Bullingbrook is chang'd.
You must to Pomfret, not unto the Tower.
And, madam, there is order ta'en for you.
With all swift speed you must away to France.

Richard

55 Northumberland, thou ladder wherewithal
The mounting Bullingbrook ascends my throne,
The time shall not be many hours of age
More than it is ere foul sin gathering head
Shall break into corruption. Thou shalt think
60 Though he divide the realm and give thee half
It is too little, helping him to all.
He shall think that thou which knowest the way
To plant unrightful kings wilt know again,
Being ne'er so little urg'd, another way
65 To pluck him headlong from the usurped throne.
The love of wicked men converts to fear,
That fear to hate, and hate turns one or both
To worthy danger and deserved death.

Northumberland

My guilt be on my head, and there an end.
70 Take leave and part, for you must part forthwith.

Richard

Doubly divorc'd! Bad men, you violate
A twofold marriage twixt my crown and me
And then betwixt me and my married wife.
Let me unkiss the oath twixt thee and me—
75 And yet not so, for with a kiss 'twas made.
Part us, Northumberland: I towards the north
Where shivering cold and sickness pines the clime,
My wife to France, from whence set forth in pomp
She came adorned hither like sweet May,
80 Sent back like Hollowmas or short'st of day.

Queen

And must we be divided? Must we part?

Richard

Ay, hand from hand, my love, and heart from heart.

Queen

Banish us both, and send the king with me.

Northumberland

That were some love, but little policy.

Queen

85 Then whither he goes thither let me go.

Richard

So two together weeping make one woe.
Weep thou for me in France, I for thee here;
Better far off than, near, be ne'er the near.
Go, count thy way with sighs, I mine with groans.

---

58 *gathering head*: i.e. swelling up like a boil.

60 *Though he*: even though he should.
61 *helping him to all*: since you helped him to get it all.

65 *usurped*: usurpèd.

67 *one or both*: i.e. of the 'wicked men'.

68 *worthy*: justifiable.
deserved: deservèd.

69 *and there an end*: and let that be the end of it.
70 *part . . . part*: make your parting (from the queen) . . . depart.

74–5 Richard addresses the queen.
74 *unkiss the oath*: release the oath with a kiss.

77 *pines the clime*: starves the climate.
78 *pomp*: splendour.
79 Couplets characterize the grave, stylized parting of Richard and his queen.
adorned: adornèd.
80 *Hollowmas*: All Saints ('Hallows') Day, 1 November, which was regarded as the winter solstice.

88 *ne'er the near*: never any nearer together.

Queen
90 So longest way shall have the longest moans.
    Richard
Twice for one step I'll groan, the way being short,
And piece the way out with a heavy heart.
Come, come, in wooing sorrow let's be brief
Since, wedding it, there is such length in grief.
95 One kiss shall stop our mouths, and dumbly part.
Thus give I mine, and thus take I thy heart.
    Queen
Give me mine own again. 'Twere no good part
To take on me to keep and kill thy heart.
So, now I have mine own again be gone,
100 That I may strive to kill it with a groan.
    Richard
We make woe wanton with this fond delay.
Once more adieu, the rest let sorrow say.

                      [*Exeunt*

92 *piece . . . out*: lengthen the journey.

95 *dumbly part*: part in silence.
96 *Thus*: i.e. with a kiss.

97-8 *'Twere . . . thy heart*: it would not be a good deed if I were to undertake to look after your heart and then kill it.

101 *wanton*: reckless, unrestrained.
fond: foolishly loving.

Scene 2

The Duke of York's *house. Enter* Duke of
York *and the* Duchess

    Duchess
My lord, you told me you would tell the rest,
When weeping made you break the story off,
Of our two cousins coming into London.
    York
Where did I leave?
    Duchess
                At that sad stop, my lord,
5 Where rude misgovern'd hands from windows' tops
Threw dust and rubbish on King Richard's head.
    York
Then, as I said, the duke, great Bullingbrook,
Mounted upon a hot and fiery steed
Which his aspiring rider seem'd to know,
10 With slow but stately pace kept on his course,
Whilst all tongues cried 'God save thee,
    Bullingbrook!'
You would have thought the very windows spake,
So many greedy looks of young and old

Act 5   Scene 2

The Duke of York describes Bullingbrook's triumphant entry into London and then learns about his son's part in the conspiracy to murder Bullingbrook.

3 *cousins*: nephews.

5 *rude*: brutal.
windows' tops: high windows.

7 *Bullingbrook*: The entry into London preceded the coronation.

9 *his aspiring . . . know*: seemed to know the ambitious rider.

Through casements darted their desiring eyes
15 Upon his visage, and that all the walls
With painted imagery had said at once
'Jesu preserve thee! Welcome, Bullingbrook!'
Whilst he from one side to the other turning,
Bare headed, lower than his proud steed's neck,
20 Bespake them thus: 'I thank you, countrymen',
And thus still doing, thus he pass'd along.
     Duchess
Alack, poor Richard. Where rode he the whilst?
     York
As in a theatre the eyes of men
After a well-grac'd actor leaves the stage
25 Are idly bent on him that enters next,
Thinking his prattle to be tedious,
Even so or with much more contempt men's eyes
Did scowl on Richard. No man cried 'God save him',
No joyful tongue gave him his welcome home,
30 But dust was thrown upon his sacred head,
Which with such gentle sorrow he shook off,
His face still combating with tears and smiles,
The badges of his grief and patience,
That had not God for some strong purpose steel'd
35 The hearts of men they must perforce have melted
And barbarism itself have pitied him.
But heaven hath a hand in these events,
To whose high will we bound our calm contents.
To Bullingbrook are we sworn subjects now,
40 Whose state and honour I for aye allow.

          Enter Aumerle

     Duchess
Here comes my son Aumerle.
     York
                              Aumerle that was,
But that is lost for being Richard's friend,
And, madam, you must call him Rutland now.
I am in Parliament pledge for his truth
45 And lasting fealty to the new-made king.
     Duchess
Welcome, my son. Who are the violets now
That strew the green lap of the new-come spring?

16 *painted imagery*: York refers to the wall-
hangings in Elizabethan houses—painted
cloths with characters portrayed, as in
strip-cartoons, with sentences issuing
from their mouths.
     at once: all together.
19 *lower*: i.e. bowing down lower from.
20 *Bespake*: addressed.
21 *still*: continually, all the time.
24 *well-grac'd*: accomplished, popular.
25 *idly*: indifferently, listlessly.
27 *Even*: The word is pronounced with one
syllable, 'e'en'.
33 *badges*: insignia, outward signs (of a
noble soul).
36 *barbarism itself*: even savages.
38 *bound . . . contents*: submit ourselves in
resignation: the rhyme with 'events'
seems to indicate York's acquiescence.
     Bullingbrook: York still insists on using
the name, and not the title 'king'.
41–2 *Aumerle . . . friend*: The Dukes of
Aumerle, Surrey, and Exeter were given
these titles by Richard—and were
deprived of them at the abdication.
44 *truth*: loyalty.
45 *fealty*: faithfulness.
     new-made: York is emphatic that
Bullingbrook has not achieved the
crown through birth or succession.
46–7 *violets . . . spring*: i.e. favourites in the
new court.

49 *had as lief*: would rather.

50 *bear you well*: conduct yourself
honourably.

52 *Do . . . hold*: are the plans for these
tournaments going ahead.

56 *seal . . . bosom*: According to Holinshed,
Aumerle carried the document inside
his shirt, but the attached seal hung
down outside.

60 *pardon me*: i.e. forgive me if I don't show
you the document.

65 *band*: bond; York picks up the word and
plays with different senses in the next
lines.
66 *'gainst*: in preparation for.
67 *Bound to himself*: A bond acknowledging
debt would be in possession of the
creditor, not the debtor.
69 *Boy*: A reminder of the filial duty owed
to York.

Aumerle
Madam, I know not, nor I greatly care not.
God knows I had as lief be none as one.
York
50 Well, bear you well in this new spring of time
Lest you be cropped before you come to prime.
What news from Oxford? Do these jousts and
    triumphs hold?
Aumerle
For aught I know, my lord, they do.
York
You will be there, I know.
Aumerle
55 If God prevent it not I purpose so.
York
What seal is that that hangs without thy bosom?
Yea, lookst thou pale? Let me see the writing.
Aumerle
My lord, 'tis nothing.
York
                            No matter then who see it.
I will be satisfied. Let me see the writing.
Aumerle
60 I do beseech your grace to pardon me.
It is a matter of small consequence,
Which for some reasons I would not have seen.
York
Which for some reasons, sir, I mean to see.
I fear, I fear—
Duchess
                        What should you fear?
65 'Tis nothing but some band that he is enter'd into
For gay apparel 'gainst the triumph day.
York
Bound to himself? What doth he with a bond
That he is bound to? Wife, thou art a fool.
Boy, let me see the writing.
Aumerle
70 I do beseech you pardon me. I may not show it.
York
I will be satisfied. Let me see it, I say.

He plucks it out of his bosom and reads it

York
Treason, foul treason! Villain! Traitor! Slave!
Duchess
What's the matter, my lord?
York
Ho, who's within there? Saddle my horse!
75 God for His mercy, what treachery is here!
Duchess
Why, what is't, my lord?
York
Give me my boots, I say! Saddle my horse!
Now by mine honour, by my life, my troth,
I will appeach the villain.
Duchess
                     What is the matter?
York
80 Peace, foolish woman!
Duchess
I will not peace. What is the matter, Aumerle?
Aumerle
Good mother, be content. It is no more
Than my poor life must answer.
Duchess
                     Thy life answer?
York
Bring me my boots! I will unto the king.

His man enters with his boots

Duchess
85 Strike him, Aumerle! Poor boy, thou art amaz'd.
Hence, villain! Never more come in my sight.
York
Give me my boots, I say.
Duchess
                 Why, York, what wilt thou do?
Wilt thou not hide the trespass of thine own?
Have we more sons, or are we like to have?
90 Is not my teeming date drunk up with time,
And wilt thou pluck my fair son from mine age
And rob me of a happy mother's name?
Is he not like thee? Is he not thine own?

---

75 *God . . . mercy*: may God have mercy on us.

79 *appeach*: inform against, publicly denounce.

81 *Aumerle*: The Duchess continues to use this name for her son.

85 *Strike him*: i.e. strike the servant bringing the boots.
amaz'd: bewildered, confused.

90 *teeming date*: time for bearing children.

94 *fond*: foolish.

York

Thou fond mad woman,

95 Wilt thou conceal this dark conspiracy?

A dozen of them here have ta'en the sacrament

And interchangeably set down their hands

To kill the king at Oxford.

Duchess

He shall be none.

We'll keep him here, then what is that to him?

York

100 Away, fond woman! Were he twenty times my son

I would appeach him.

Duchess

Hadst thou groan'd for him

As I have done thou wouldst be more pitiful.

But now I know thy mind—thou dost suspect

That I have been disloyal to thy bed

105 And that he is a bastard, not thy son.

Sweet York, sweet husband, be not of that mind.

He is as like thee as a man may be,

Not like to me or any of my kin,

And yet I love him.

York

Make way, unruly woman!   [*Exit*

Duchess

110 After, Aumerle! Mount thee upon his horse,

Spur post, and get before him to the king

And beg thy pardon ere he do accuse thee.

I'll not be long behind. Though I be old

I doubt not but to ride as fast as York,

115 And never will I rise up from the ground

Till Bullingbrook have pardon'd thee. Away, be gone.

[*Exeunt*

96 *ta'en the sacrament*: received Holy Communion to seal their promise (see 4, 1, 327).

97 *interchangeably . . . hands*: signed reciprocally (so that each could have a copy).

98 *be none*: not be one of them.

101 *groan'd*: suffered the pains of childbirth.

111 *Spur post*: set spurs to the horse and hurry.

Act 5   Scene 3

The York family—son, father, and mother—
tell Bullingbrook about the conspiracy to
murder him.

1 *unthrifty*: spendthrift, profligate.
3 *any plague*: Bullingbrook perhaps
remembers Richard's threat of 'Armies
of pestilence' (*3, 3, 87*).
hang over: It was popularly believed that
the plague was sent by heaven and fell
down from the clouds.

7 *unrestrained*: unrestrainèd.

9 *watch*: night watchmen.
passengers: travellers.
10 *wanton*: reckless.
11 *Takes . . . honour*: makes it a point of
honour.

14 *held*: to be held.

15 *the gallant*: his lordship. The word,
spoken sarcastically, is accented on the
second syllable.
16 *the stews*: the brothel quarter, the 'red
light district'.

Scene 3

Windsor Castle. Enter Bullingbrook *as*
king, Percy *and other* Lords

Bullingbrook
Can no man tell of my unthrifty son?
'Tis full three months since I did see him last.
If any plague hang over us 'tis he.
I would to God, my lords, he might be found.
5 Enquire at London 'mongst the taverns there,
For there they say he daily doth frequent
With unrestrained loose companions,
Even such, they say, as stand in narrow lanes
And beat our watch and rob our passengers,
10 Whilst he, young, wanton and effeminate boy,
Takes on the point of honour to support
So dissolute a crew.
    Percy
My lord, some two days since I saw the prince
And told him of those triumphs held at Oxford.
    Bullingbrook
15 And what said the gallant?
    Percy
His answer was he would unto the stews
And from the commonest creature pluck a glove

18 *favour*: token of allegiance—like the
gauntlets thrown down as 'gages' in
Act 1, Scene 1 and *Act 4*, Scene 1.

22 *happily*: with any luck, hopefully.

23s.d. *amazed*: in confusion, distraught.

And wear it as a favour, and with that
He would unhorse the lustiest challenger.
    Bullingbrook
20 As dissolute as desperate! Yet through both
I see some sparks of better hope in him
Which elder years may happily bring forth.
But who comes here?

        Enter Aumerle *amazed*

    Aumerle
                Where is the king?
    Bullingbrook
                    What means
Our cousin, that he stares and looks so wildly?
    Aumerle
25 God save your grace. I do beseech your majesty
To have some conference with your grace alone.
    Bullingbrook
Withdraw yourselves, and leave us here alone.
                [Exeunt Percy *and* Lords
What is the matter with our cousin now?
    Aumerle
For ever may my knees grow to the earth, *[Kneels]*

30 *My tongue . . . mouth*: 'let my tongue
cleave to the roof of my mouth'
(Psalm 137:6).
31 *Unless a pardon*: Aumerle is breathless
and gabbles out his words.
33 *on the first*: i.e. 'intended' (but not
'committed').
34 *win thy after love*: gratitude and future
loyalty.

30 My tongue cleave to the roof within my mouth,
Unless a pardon ere I rise or speak.
    Bullingbrook
Intended or committed was this fault?
If on the first, how heinous e'er it be
To win thy after love I pardon thee.
    Aumerle
35 *[Rises]* Then give me leave that I may turn the key
That no man enter till my tale be done.
    Bullingbrook
Have thy desire.

       The Duke of York *knocks at the door
       and crieth*

    York
[Within] My liege, beware, look to thyself.
Thou hast a traitor in thy presence there.

40 *I'll . . . safe*: I'll render you harmless (by killing him).

Bullingbrook

40 Villain, I'll make thee safe.

Draws his sword

Aumerle

Stay thy revengeful hand. Thou hast no cause to fear.

York

42 *secure*: overconfident, complacent.

43 *for love . . . treason*: out of my love for you call you a fool.

[*Within*] Open the door, secure foolhardy king.
Shall I for love speak treason to thy face?
Open the door or I will break it open!

Enter York

Bullingbrook

45 What is the matter, uncle? Speak.
Recover breath. Tell us how near is danger,
That we may arm us to encounter it.

York

[*Hands him a document*] Peruse this writing here
   and thou shalt know

49 *my haste*: i.e. breathlessness as a result of haste.

The treason that my haste forbids me show.

Aumerle

50 *thy promise past*: the promise you have given.

50 Remember, as thou read'st, thy promise past.
I do repent me. Read not my name there.
My heart is not confederate with my hand.

52 *confederate*: in league.

York

53 *set it down*: sign it.

It was, villain, ere thy hand did set it down.
I tore it from the traitor's bosom, king.
55 Fear and not love begets his penitence.
Forget to pity him, lest thy pity prove

56 *to pity*: i.e. your promise to pity.
56-7 *pity . . . heart*: York's metaphor evokes Richard's image of the deadly snake cherished in the bosom (see *3, 2, 131*).

A serpent that will sting thee to the heart.

Bullingbrook

Oh heinous, strong, and bold conspiracy!
Oh loyal father of a treacherous son!

60 *sheer*: pure.
62 *held his current*: flowed.
63 *converts to bad*: changes to bad (in Aumerle).
65 *deadly*: (a) murderous; (b) fatal.
   blot: flaw, sin—and, literally, signature on the paper.
   digressing: (a) divergent; (b) transgressing.
66 *be . . . bawd*: serve his wickedness like a brothel-keeper.
67 *spend*: (a) expend (semen); (b) squander (money).

60 Thou sheer, immaculate, and silver fountain,
From whence this stream through muddy passages
Hath held his current and defil'd himself,
Thy overflow of good converts to bad,
And thy abundant goodness shall excuse
65 This deadly blot in thy digressing son.

York

So shall my virtue be his vice's bawd
And he shall spend mine honour with his shame,

69 *his dishonour dies*: i.e. he dies himself.

70 *Or*: or else.

71 *in his life*: i.e. by allowing him to live.

74–9 The rhyming couplets combine with the hammering at the door and the many kneelings to bring this scene very near to farce—as Bullingbrook appreciates!

79 *'The Beggar . . . King'*: Bullingbrook refers to the story of King Cophetua and the Beggar Maid, popular in ballad form or as a stage version.

84–5 *This fester'd joint . . . confound*: York recommends amputation for the gangrenous limb so that the disease will not spread through the body politic.

85 *let alone*: left untreated.
   confound: infect, destroy.

87 *Love . . . can*: i.e. if York can't love his own son (who is a part of himself) then he must be incapable of loving anyone else.

88 *make*: do.

89 *dugs*: breasts.
   once more . . . 'rear: give life for a second time to a traitor.

92 *walk upon my knees*: A traditional form of penance.

94 *bid me joy*: tell me to be joyful.

95 *Rutland*: The Duchess can appreciate that the title 'Aumerle' would be tactless here.

As thriftless sons their scraping fathers' gold.
Mine honour lives when his dishonour dies,
70 Or my sham'd life in his dishonour lies.
Thou kill'st me in his life. Giving him breath
The traitor lives, the true man's put to death.
         Duchess
[*Within*] What ho, my liege! For God's sake let me in!
         Bullingbrook
What shrill-voic'd suppliant makes this eager cry?
         Duchess
75 [*Within*] A woman and thy aunt, great king. 'Tis I.
Speak with me, pity me, open the door!
A beggar begs that never begg'd before.
         Bullingbrook
Our scene is alter'd from a serious thing,
And now chang'd to 'The Beggar and the King'.
80 My dangerous cousin, let your mother in.
I know she's come to pray for your foul sin.
         York
If thou do pardon whosoever pray,
More sins for this forgiveness prosper may.
This fester'd joint cut off, the rest rest sound.
85 This let alone will all the rest confound.

                Enter Duchess

         Duchess
Oh, king, believe not this hard-hearted man.
Love loving not itself none other can.
         York
Thou frantic woman, what dost thou make here?
Shall thy old dugs once more a traitor rear?
         Duchess
90 Sweet York, be patient. Hear me, gentle liege.
   [*Kneels*]
         Bullingbrook
Rise up, good aunt.
         Duchess
                    Not yet, I thee beseech.
For ever will I walk upon my knees
And never see day that the happy sees
Till thou give joy, until thou bid me joy
95 By pardoning Rutland, my transgressing boy.

Aumerle

Unto my mother's prayers I bend my knee. [*Kneels*]

York

Against them both my true joints bended be. [*Kneels*]
Ill mayst thou thrive if thou grant any grace.

Duchess

Pleads he in earnest? Look upon his face.

100 His eyes do drop no tears, his prayers are in jest,
His words come from his mouth, ours from our
      breast.
He prays but faintly, and would be denied.
We pray with heart and soul and all beside.
His weary joints would gladly rise, I know.

105 Our knees still kneel till to the ground they grow.
His prayers are full of false hypocrisy,
Ours of true zeal and deep integrity.
Our prayers do outpray his—then let them have
That mercy which true prayer ought to have.

Bullingbrook

110 Good aunt, stand up.

Duchess

                                Nay, do not say 'stand up',
Say 'pardon' first, and afterwards 'stand up'.
And if I were thy nurse thy tongue to teach
'Pardon' should be the first word of thy speech.
I never long'd to hear a word till now.

115 Say 'pardon', king. Let pity teach thee how.
The word is short, but not so short as sweet.
No word like 'pardon' for kings' mouths so meet.

York

Speak it in French, king. Say 'pardonne moy'.

Duchess

Dost thou teach pardon pardon to destroy?

120 Ah, my sour husband, my hard-hearted lord,
That sets the word itself against the word,
Speak 'pardon' as 'tis current in our land.
The chopping French we do not understand.
Thine eye begins to speak—set thy tongue there,

125 Or in thy piteous heart plant thou thine ear
That, hearing how our plaints and prayers do pierce,
Pity may move thee 'pardon' to rehearse.

100 *in jest*: playful.

102 *would be denied*: wants to be refused.

105 *still kneel*: will kneel perpetually.

112 *And if*: if only.

117 *meet*: proper, appropriate.

118 *'pardonne moy'*: excuse me—i.e. for *not*
speaking a pardon for Aumerle.

119 *teach . . . destroy*: i.e. by using the word
against itself.

123 *chopping*: logic chopping, shifting
meanings; the French philosopher Peter
Ramus was especially famous for this
kind of argument.

126 *plaints*: laments.
pierce: The word is pronounced to
rhyme with 'rehearse'.

127 *rehearse*: recite, repeat (the Duchess
continues the image of language
teaching from lines 112–13).

129 *suit . . . hand*: (a) plea I am making;
(b) cards I am holding.

131 *happy*: fortunate.
vantage: advantage, perspective.

133 *Twice saying . . . twain*: to say 'pardon'
twice will not split the pardon in two.

136 *But for*: but as for.
trusty: trustworthy (Bullingbrook is
sarcastic).
brother-in-law: i.e. the Duke of Exeter
(referred to at *2*, *1*, *281*).
abbot: i.e. the Abbot of Westminster.
137 *consorted crew*: gang who have joined
with them.
138 *straight*: immediately.
139 *several*: separate.
powers: forces.
144 *prove you*: may you prove, you must
prove.
145 *old*: former—i.e. reclaimed from his
lapse into disloyalty.
I pray . . . new: 'grant that . . . the new
man may be raised up in him' (Baptism
service, Book of Common Prayer).

Bullingbrook
Good aunt, stand up.
Duchess
                                    I do not sue to stand.
Pardon is all the suit I have in hand.
Bullingbrook
130 I pardon him, as God shall pardon me.
Duchess
Oh happy vantage of a kneeling knee!
Yet am I sick for fear. Speak it again.
Twice saying 'pardon' doth not pardon twain,
But makes one pardon strong.
Bullingbrook
                                    With all my heart
135 I pardon him.
Duchess
                        A god on earth thou art.
Bullingbrook
But for our trusty brother-in-law and the abbot,
With all the rest of that consorted crew,
Destruction straight shall dog them at the heels.
Good uncle, help to order several powers
140 To Oxford or where'er these traitors are.
They shall not live within this world, I swear,
But I will have them if I once know where.
Uncle, farewell, and cousin too adieu.
Your mother well hath pray'd, and prove you true.
Duchess
145 Come, my old son. I pray God make thee new.
                                                [Exeunt

Act 5   Scene 4

Exton prepares to do the will of Bullingbrook.

5 *urg'd it*: insisted on it.

7 *wishtly*: longingly, intently.

11 *rid*: get rid of.

Scene 4

Windsor Castle. Enter Exton *and* Servants

Exton
Didst thou not mark the king, what words he
    spake?
'Have I no friend will rid me of this living fear?'
Was it not so?
Servant   These were his very words.
Exton
'Have I no friend?' quoth he. He spake it twice,
5 And urg'd it twice together, did he not?
Servant
He did.
Exton
And speaking it, he wishtly look'd on me
As who should say 'I would thou wert the man
That would divorce this terror from my heart',
10 Meaning the king at Pomfret. Come, let's go.
I am the king's friend, and will rid his foe.
                                        [*Exeunt*

Act 5   Scene 5

Alone in prison, Richard is attempting to
create a whole world in his own mind when
he is visited by a faithful groom. But the visit
is cut short by Exton and his servants, who
come to murder the king.

3 *for because*: because.

5 *hammer't out*: puzzle it out.

8 *generation*: family, offspring.
  still breeding: endlessly reproducing.
9 *this little world*: i.e. the prison.
10 *humours*: temperaments.

Scene 5

The prison at Pomfret Castle. Enter Richard
alone

Richard
I have been studying how I may compare
This prison where I live unto the world,
And for because the world is populous
And here is not a creature but myself
5 I cannot do it. Yet I'll hammer't out.
My brain I'll prove the female to my soul,
My soul the father, and these two beget
A generation of still breeding thoughts,
And these same thoughts people this little world
10 In humours like the people of this world,
For no thought is contented. The better sort,

13 *scruples*: niggling little doubts.

13–14 *do set . . . the word*: even find
passages from the Bible (= the word of
God) which contradict each other. The
Duchess has already accused York of
this (5, 3, 121).

15 *'Come, little ones'*: 'Jesus said, "Suffer
little children . . . to come unto me" '
(Matthew 19:14).

16–17 *'It is as hard . . . eye'*: 'It is easier for
a camel to go through the eye of a
needle, than for a rich man to enter into
the kingdom of God' (Matthew 19:24).
This second passage already seems to
contain a play on words with 'camel'
(= cable rope) and 'needle' (= door for
pedestrians in a city gate), and
Shakespeare extends the play with his
'thread' and 'postern'.

17 *postern*: little back gate.

needle: The word is pronounced as a
monosyllable, 'neele'.

20 *ribs*: framework (of castle and of man).

21 *ragged*: rugged, jagged.

22 *for*: because.
   in their own pride: of frustrated ambition.

23 *tending to content*: persuading to
acceptance and Christian patience.

25 *silly*: simple-minded, foolish.

26 *refuge*: console, take shelter from.

27 *set*: sit, be set.

33 *treasons*: i.e. the thought of treasons.

39 *but man is*: is only a man.

42 *Ha, ha*: Richard detects a fault in the
rhythm.

43 *time . . . kept*: rhythm is faulty and the
correct note values are not observed.

46 *check*: rebuke.
   string: string instrument.

47 *concord*: harmony.

48 *my true time broke*: the discord in my
own affairs.

49 *waste me*: cause me to waste away.

As thoughts of things divine, are intermix'd
With scruples, and do set the word itself
Against the word—
15 As thus: 'Come, little ones', and then again
'It is as hard to come as for a camel
To thread the postern of a small needle's eye.'
Thoughts tending to ambition, they do plot
Unlikely wonders: how these vain weak nails
20 May tear a passage through the flinty ribs
Of this hard world my ragged prison walls,
And, for they cannot, die in their own pride.
Thoughts tending to content flatter themselves
That they are not the first of Fortune's slaves,
25 Nor shall not be the last, like silly beggars
Who, sitting in the stocks, refuge their shame
That many have and others must set there,
And in this thought they find a kind of ease,
Bearing their own misfortunes on the back
30 Of such as have before endur'd the like.
Thus play I in one person many people,
And none contented. Sometimes am I king,
Then treasons make me wish myself a beggar,
And so I am. Then crushing penury
35 Persuades me I was better when a king,
Then am I king'd again, and by and by
Think that I am unking'd by Bullingbrook,
And straight am nothing. But whate'er I be
Nor I nor any man that but man is
40 With nothing shall be pleas'd till he be eas'd
With being nothing.

The music plays

Music do I hear?
Ha, ha, keep time! How sour sweet music is
When time is broke and no proportion kept.
So is it in the music of men's lives.
45 And here have I the daintiness of ear
To check time broke in a disorder'd string,
But for the concord of my state and time
Had not an ear to hear my true time broke.
I wasted time and now doth time waste me,

50–4 *now . . . tears*: Musical time leads Richard's fancy to chronological time and he compares himself to a clock: his thoughts are minutes, driven by sighs from one mark to the next on the clock-face—his eyes—to which his finger, like the hand of a dial, is always pointing as it wipes away his tears.

51 *jar*: knock themselves onwards.

52 *watches*: intervals, periods of waking time.
outward watch: clock-face—*and also* sentry on guard.

53 *dial's point*: hand on clock-face.

54 *still*: (a) continually; (b) motionless.

55 *Now, sir*: Richard imagines himself with a listener.

58 *times*: i.e. quarters and half hours.
my time: i.e. time on earth; Richard suspects that his life may soon be coming to an end.

59 *posting*: speeding.

60 *his Jack of the clock*: Whilst triumphant Bullingbrook speeds ahead, Richard is left behind to number the hours like the little man who strikes the bell.

61 *mads*: drives me mad.

62 *have holp*: may have helped.
madmen . . . wits: Music has long been recognized as therapy for the mentally disturbed.

66 *brooch*: rare jewel.

67–8 *royal . . . noble . . . groats*: Richard puns on the names of three coins: two 'royals' were equivalent to £1, and so were three 'nobles'; ten 'groats' was the difference between them.

67 *peer*: lord—and 'equal'.

68 *cheapest*: i.e. the cheaper of us, Richard himself: to call him 'royal' is to price him too high by ten groats.

70 *sad dog*: miserable fellow.

75 *sometime royal*: formerly royal.

76 *ern'd*: grieved.

77 *coronation day*: This was 13 October 1399.

78 *roan*: of mixed colour.

50 For now hath time made me his numbering clock.
My thoughts are minutes, and with sighs they jar
Their watches on unto mine eyes, the outward watch,
Whereto my finger like a dial's point
Is pointing still, in cleansing them from tears.
55 Now, sir, the sound that tells what hour it is
Are clamorous groans that strike upon my heart,
Which is the bell. So sighs and tears and groans
Show minutes, times, and hours. But my time
Runs posting on in Bullingbrook's proud joy
60 While I stand fooling here, his Jack of the clock.
This music mads me. Let it sound no more,
For though it have holp madmen to their wits
In me it seems it will make wise men mad.
Yet blessing on his heart that gives it me,
65 For 'tis a sign of love, and love to Richard
Is a strange brooch in this all-hating world.

Enter a Groom *of the stable*

Groom
Hail, royal prince!
　　　　　　Richard
　　　　　　　　　　Thanks, noble peer.
The cheapest of us is ten groats too dear.
What art thou? And how comest thou hither
70 Where no man never comes but that sad dog
That brings me food to make misfortune live?
　　　　Groom
I was a poor groom of thy stable, king,
When thou wert king, who, travelling towards York,
With much ado at length have gotten leave
75 To look upon my sometime royal master's face.
Oh, how it ern'd my heart when I beheld
In London streets that coronation day
When Bullingbrook rode on roan Barbary,
That horse that thou so often hast bestrid,
80 That horse that I so carefully have dress'd.
　　　　Richard
Rode he on Barbary? Tell me, gentle friend,
How went he under him?

Groom

So proudly as if he disdain'd the ground.

Richard

So proud that Bullingbrook was on his back.

85 That jade hath ate bread from my royal hand,
This hand hath made him proud with clapping him.
Would he not stumble, would he not fall down,
Since pride must have a fall, and break the neck
Of that proud man that did usurp his back?
90 Forgiveness! Horse, why do I rail on thee,
Since thou, created to be aw'd by man,
Wast born to bear? I was not made a horse
And yet I bear a burthen like an ass,
Spurr'd, gall'd, and tir'd by jauncing Bullingbrook.

Enter Keeper *to* Richard *with meat*

Keeper

95 Fellow, give place. Here is no longer stay.

Richard

If thou love me 'tis time thou wert away.

Groom

What my tongue dares not, that my heart shall say.
[*Exit*

Keeper

My lord, wilt please you to fall to?

Richard

Taste of it first as thou art wont to do.

Keeper

100 My lord, I dare not. Sir Pierce of Exton,
Who lately came from the king, commands the
contrary.

Richard

The devil take Henry of Lancaster, and thee!
Patience is stale, and I am weary of it!

Beats the Keeper

Keeper

Help, help, help!

The murderers, Exton *and* Servants, *rush in*

---

85 *jade*: nag, vicious horse.
86 *clapping*: patting.

88 *pride must have a fall*: 'Pride goeth before destruction; and a haughty spirit before a fall' (Proverbs 16:18).
90 *rail on*: swear about.
93 *burthen*: An alternative spelling of 'burden'.

94 *gall'd*: made sore.
jauncing: prancing (moving up and down with the horse's movements).

95 *Fellow*: The keeper addresses the groom according to his status.
98 *fall to*: eat your meal.

99 *Taste . . . do*: It was usual for food to be tasted in front of the king to detect any poison.
wont: accustomed.

105 *What . . . assault*: how dare you try this crude way of killing me.

107 *room*: place.

109 *staggers*: makes stagger, dislodges.

116 *chronicl'd in hell*: written among the deeds of the damned.

Richard

105 How now! What means death in this rude assault?
Villain, thy own hand yields thy death's instrument.
Go thou and fill another room in hell.

Here Exton *strikes him down*

That hand shall burn in never-quenching fire
That staggers thus my person. Exton, thy fierce hand
110 Hath with the king's blood stain'd the king's own land.
Mount, mount my soul. Thy seat is up on high
Whilst my gross flesh sinks downward, here to die.
    [*Dies*]
    Exton
As full of valour as of royal blood.
Both have I spill'd. Oh, would the deed were good,
115 For now the devil that told me I did well
Says that this deed is chronicl'd in hell.
This dead king to the living king I'll bear.
Take hence the rest and give them burial here.
                                              [*Exeunt*

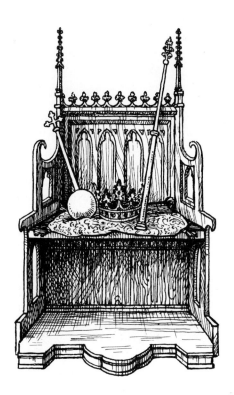

Act 5   Scene 6

Bullingbrook, now King Henry IV, listens with satisfaction to the news of his party's successes; Exton brings in the body of King Richard.

os.d. *Flourish*: The stage direction for a fanfare of trumpets enforces the point that Bullingbrook is king.

3   *Ciceter*: Cirencester. The modern word still has this pronunciation.

6   *sacred state*: Northumberland salutes the throne, symbolic chair of state, rather than Bullingbrook himself.

7–8 *The next news . . . Kent*: 'the heads of the chief conspirators were set on poles over London Bridge, to the terror of others' (Holinshed).

Scene 6

Windsor Castle. Flourish. Enter Bullingbrook, York, *with other* Lords *and* Attendants

Bullingbrook
Kind uncle York, the latest news we hear
Is that the rebels have consum'd with fire
Our town of Ciceter in Gloucestershire,
But whether they be ta'en or slain we hear not.

Enter Northumberland

5 Welcome, my lord. What is the news?
Northumberland
First, to thy sacred state wish I all happiness.
The next news is I have to London sent
The heads of Salisbury, Spencer, Blunt, and Kent.
The manner of their taking may appear

10 *At large discoursed*: discoursèd; described in full.

12 *right worthy*: (a) well-merited; (b) very substantial.

15 *consorted*: associated.

19 *The grand conspirator*: i.e. the Abbot of Westminster.
20 *clog*: burden.
    sour: bitter.

23 *doom*: condemnation.

25 *secret*: secluded.
    reverend room: monastic dwelling-place.
26 *More . . . hast*: more worthy of reverence than what you have now (i.e. his prison cell).
    joy: enjoy.

33 *Richard of Bordeaux*: Exton will not use the title 'King'.

35 *A . . . slander*: a deed of murder which will cast slander.

---

10 At large discoursed in this paper here.

Bullingbrook
We thank thee, gentle Percy, for thy pains,
And to thy worth will add right worthy gains.

Enter Lord Fitzwater

Fitzwater
My lord, I have from Oxford sent to London
The heads of Broccas and Sir Bennet Seely,
15 Two of the dangerous consorted traitors
That sought at Oxford thy dire overthrow.

Bullingbrook
Thy pains, Fitzwater, shall not be forgot.
Right noble is thy merit, well I wot.

Enter Percy *and* Carlisle

Percy
The grand conspirator, Abbot of Westminster,
20 With clog of conscience and sour melancholy
Hath yielded up his body to the grave.
But here is Carlisle living, to abide
Thy kingly doom and sentence of his pride.

Bullingbrook
Carlisle, this is your doom:
25 Choose out some secret place, some reverend room,
More than thou hast, and with it joy thy life.
So, as thou livest in peace die free from strife.
For though mine enemy thou hast ever been
High sparks of honour in thee have I seen.

Enter Exton *with a coffin*

Exton
30 Great king, within this coffin I present
Thy buried fear. Herein all breathless lies
The mightiest of thy greatest enemies,
Richard of Bordeaux, by me hither brought.

Bullingbrook
Exton, I thank thee not, for thou hast wrought
35 A deed of slander with thy fatal hand
Upon my head and all this famous land.

Exton
From your own mouth, my lord, did I this deed.

Bullingbrook
They love not poison that do poison need.
Nor do I thee. Though I did wish him dead,
40 I hate the murderer, love him murdered.
The guilt of conscience take thou for thy labour,
But neither my good word nor princely favour.
With Cain go wander through shades of night
And never show thy head by day nor light.
45 Lords, I protest my soul is full of woe
That blood should sprinkle me to make me grow.
Come mourn with me for what I do lament,
And put on sullen black incontinent.
I'll make a voyage to the Holy Land
50 To wash this blood off from my guilty hand.
March sadly after. Grace my mournings here
In weeping after this untimely bier.   [*Exeunt*

40 *murdered*: murderèd.
41 *guilt of conscience*: guilty conscience (and not the 'gilt' of payment in gold).
43 *With Cain*: For the murder of his brother Abel, Cain was condemned to be 'a fugitive and a vagabond . . . in the earth' (Genesis 4:12). See *1, 1, 104*.
46 *sprinkle me*: be sprinkled on me.
48 *incontinent*: immediately.
49 *voyage*: pilgrimage.
51 *Grace*: honour with your presence.
52 *untimely bier*: premature death.

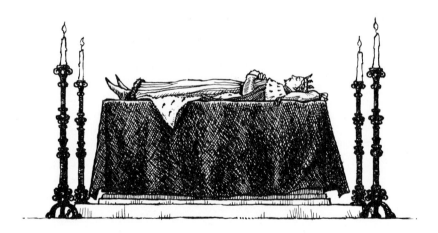

Shakespeare's Sources

It would be futile to attempt a comprehensive survey of Shakespeare's source material in a volume such as this one, but the passages presented here may offer some slight insight into the dramatist's careful and *creative* reading. (See also 'Source, Date, and Text', p. xxxi.)

Act I, Scene 4, lines 24–48

24 *his courtship to the common people*
. . . A wonder it was to see what number of people ran after him in every town and street where he came before he took the sea, lamenting and bewailing his departure, as who would say that when he departed the only shield, defence, and comfort of the commonwealth was vaded and gone . . .

Holinshed[1]

. . . and always as he rode he inclined his head to the people on every side.

Froissart[2]

38 *the rebels which stand out in Ireland*
. . . the King being advertised that the wild Irish daily wasted and destroyed the towns and villages within the English pale, and had slain many of the soldiers which lay there in garrison for defence of that country, determined to make eftsoons a voyage thither, and prepared all things necessary for his passage now against the spring . . . and so in the month of April, as divers authors write, he set forward from Windsor . . .

Holinshed

45 *We are enforc'd to farm our royal realm*
    We shall be censured strangely, when they tell
    How our great father toiled his royal person

---

[1] Raphael Holinshed, *Chronicles of England, Scotland, and Ireland* (2nd edition, 1574).
[2] *The Chronicle of Froissart translated out of French* by Sir John Bourchier, Lord Berners (1523–5).

Spending his blood to purchase towns in France;
And we his son, to ease our wanton youth
Become a landlord to this warlike realm,
Rent out our kingdom like a pelting farm

Woodstock, IV, i, 142–7

48 *Our substitutes at home shall have blank charters*
These blank charters shall be forthwith sent
To every shrieve through all the shires of England,
With charge to call before them presently
All landed men, freeholders, farmers, graziers,
Or any else that have ability.
Then in your highness' name they shall be charged
To set their names, and forthwith seal these blanks . . .

Woodstock, III, i, 16–24

These gentlemen here, Sir Henry Greene, Sir Edward Bagot, Sir William Bushy and Sir Thomas Scroope all jointly here stand bound to pay your majesty, or your deputy, wherever you remain, seven thousand pounds a month for this your kingdom; for which your grace, by these writings, surrenders to their hands: all your crown lands, lordships: manors, rents: taxes, subsidies, fifteens, imposts; foreign customs, staples for wool, tin, lead and cloth: all forfeitures of goods or lands confiscate; and all other duties that do, shall, or may appertain to the king or crown's revenues; and for non-payment of the sum or sums aforesaid, your majesty to seize the lands and goods of the said gentlemen above named, and their bodies to be imprisoned at your grace's pleasure.

Woodstock, IV, i, 180–93

Act 2, Scene 1, lines 201–7

201 *wrongfully seize Herford's rights*
The death of this duke [Lancaster] gave occasion of increasing more hatred in the people of this realm towards the King, for he seized into his hands all the goods that belonged to him, and also received all the rents and revenues of his lands which ought to have descended unto the Duke of Hereford by lawful inheritance, in revoking his letters patents, which he had granted him before, by virtue whereof he might make his attorneys general to sue livery for

him of any manner of inheritances or possessions that might from
thenceforth fall unto him, and that his homage might be respited
with making reasonable fine; whereby it was evident that the King
meant his utter undoing.

Holinshed

Act 5, Scene 1

1 *This way the king will come*

> 71
> Now Isabell the young afflicted Queene,
> Whose yeares had never shew'd her but delights,
> Nor lovely eies before had ever seene
> Other then smiling joies and joyfull sights:
> Borne great, matcht great, liv'd great and ever beene
> Partaker of the worlds best benefits,
> Had plac'd her selfe, hearing her Lord should passe
> That way where shee unseene in secret was.

Samuel Daniel[3]

Act 5, Scene 2, lines 3–30

3 *our two cousins coming into London*

> 69
> He that in glorie of his fortune sate,
> Admiring what he thought could never be,
> Did feele his bloud within salute his state,
> And lift up his rejoicing soule to see
> So manie hands and harts congratulate
> Th'advancement of his long desir'd degree:
> When prodegall of thankes in passing by
> He resalutes them all with cheereful eie.
> 70
> Behind him all aloofe came pensive on
> The unregarded king, that drooping went
> Alone, and but for spight scarce lookt upon,
> Judge if he did more envy or lament:
> O what a wondrous worke this daie is done,

---

[3] Samuel Daniel, *The Civil Wars Between The Two Houses Of Lancaster and York* (1595),
Book One, stanzas 69–71.

Which th'image of both fortunes doth present,
In th'one to shew the best of glories face,
In th'other worse then worst of all disgrace.

Samuel Daniel

Act 5, Scene 4

2 *'Have I no friend?'*

One writer which seemeth to have great knowledge of King
Richard's doings saith that King Henry, sitting one day at his table,
sore sighing, said 'Have I no faithful friend which will deliver me of
him, whose life will be my death, and whose death will be the
preservation of my life?' This saying was much noted of them
which were present, and especially of one called Sir Piers of Exton.
This knight incontinently departed from the court with eight
strong persons in his company, and came to Pomfret . . .

Holinshed

Act 5, Scene 5, lines 99–118

99 *Taste of it first*

Sir Piers, arrived at Pomfret, commanded the esquire that was
accustomed to sew [= serve] and take the assay before King
Richard to do so no more, saying 'Let him eat now, for he shall not
long eat.' King Richard sat down to dinner and was served without
courtesy or assay; whereupon much marvelling at the sudden
change he demanded of the esquire why he did not his duty. 'Sir,'
said he, 'I am commanded by Sir Piers of Exton, which is newly
come from King Henry.' When King Richard heard that word he
took the carving knife in his hand and strake the esquire on the
head, saying 'The devil take Henry of Lancaster and thee together.'
And with that word Sir Piers entered the chamber, well armed,
with eight tall men likewise armed, every one having a bill in his
hand.

King Richard, perceiving this, put the table from him, and
stepping to the foremost man, wrung the bill out of his hands and
so valiantly did defend himself that he slew four of those that came
thus to assail him. Sir Piers being half dismayed herewith leapt into
the chair where King Richard was wont to sit, while the other four
persons fought with him and chased him about the chamber. And
in conclusion, as King Richard traversed his ground from one side

of the chamber to another, and coming to the chair where Sir Piers stood he was felled with a stroke of the poleaxe which Sir Piers gave him upon the head, and therewith rid him out of life, without giving him respite once to call to God for mercy of his past offences. It is said that Sir Piers of Exton, after he had thus slain him, wept bitterly as one stricken with the prick of a guilty conscience for murdering him whom he had so long obeyed as king.

Holinshed

Richard II: three views on the king

Samuel Taylor Coleridge

Act I Scene 4

'In this scene a new light is thrown on Richard's character. Until now he has appeared in all the beauty of royalty; but here, as soon as he is left to himself, the inherent weakness of his character is immediately shown. It is a weakness, however, of a peculiar kind, not arising from want of personal courage, or any specific defect of faculty, but rather an intellectual feminineness which feels a necessity of ever leaning on the breast of others, and of reclining on those who are all the while known to be inferiors. To this must be attributed as its consequences all Richard's vices, his tendency to concealment, and his cunning, the whole operation of which is directed to the getting rid of present difficulties. Richard is not meant to be a debauchee; but we see in him that sophistry which is common to man, by which we can deceive our own hearts, and at one and the same time apologize for, and yet commit, the error. Shakespeare has represented this character in a very peculiar manner. He has not made him amiable with counterbalancing faults; but has openly and broadly drawn those faults without reserve, relying on Richard's disproportionate sufferings and gradually emergent good qualities for our sympathy; and this was possible, because his faults are not positive vices, but spring entirely from defect of character.'

'Marginalia and Notebooks' in *S. T. Coleridge:
Shakespeare Criticism*, ed. T. M. Raysor, vol.1 (1960)

W. B. Yeats

'I cannot believe that Shakespeare looked on his Richard II with any but sympathetic eyes, understanding indeed how ill-fitted he was to be king, at a certain moment of history, but understanding that he was lovable and full of capricious fancy, "a wild creature" as Pater has called him. The man on whom Shakespeare modelled him had been full of French elegances as he knew from Holinshed, and had given life a new luxury, a new splendour, and been "too friendly" to his friends, "too favourable" to his enemies. And certainly Shakespeare had these things in his head when he made his king fail, a little because he lacked some qualities that were doubtless common among his scullions, but more because he had certain qualities that are uncommon in all ages . . . He saw indeed, as I think, in Richard II the defeat that awaits all, whether they be artist or saint, who find themselves where men ask of them a rough energy and have nothing to give but some contemplative virtue, whether lyrical fantasy, or sweetness of temper, or dreamy dignity, or love of God, or love of His creatures. He saw that such a man through sheer bewilderment and impatience can become as unjust or as violent as any common man, any Bolingbroke or Prince John, and yet remain "that sweet lovely rose". The courtly and saintly ideals of the Middle Ages were fading, and the practical ideals of the modern age had begun to threaten the unuseful dome of the sky; Merry England was fading, and yet it was not so faded that the poets could not watch the procession of the world with that untroubled sympathy for men as they are, as apart from all they do and seem, which is the substance of tragic irony.'

'Ideas of Good and Evil' (1903), reprinted in
Essays and Introductions (1961)

Sir John Gielgud

'Richard is one of the rare parts in which the actor may indulge himself, luxuriating in the language he has to speak, and attitudinizing in consciously graceful poses. Yet the man must seem, too, to be ever physically on his guard, shielding himself, both in words and movement, from the dreaded impact of the unknown circumstances which, he feels, are always lying in wait to strike him down. He is torn between the intrinsic weakness of his nature and the pride and fastidiousness of his quality and breeding. He strives continually to retain his kingly dignity, to gain time by holding it up to the light before his enemies (as he will actually hold up to the mirror later on in the deposition scene), while he prepares inwardly to face the shock of the next humiliation. Finally, cast out into the empty darkness of his prison, he is forced to realize at last that neither his personal beauty nor the divine right of kingship can save him from inevitable horror, as he is forced to contemplate his private doom.'

'King Richard the Second', *Stage Directions* (1963)

Classwork and Examinations

The plays of Shakespeare are studied all over the world, and this classroom edition is being used in many different countries. Teaching methods vary from school to school and there are many different ways of examining a student's work. Some teachers and examiners expect detailed knowledge of Shakespeare's text; others ask for imaginative involvement with his characters and their situations; and there are some teachers who want their students, by means of 'workshop' activities, to share in the theatrical experience of directing and performing a play. Most people use a variety of methods. This section of the book offers a few suggestions for approaches to *Richard II* which could be used in schools and colleges to help with students' understanding and *enjoyment* of the play.

A Discussion
B Character Study
C Activities
D Context Questions
E Comprehension and Appreciation Questions
F Essays
G Projects

A   Discussion

Talking about the play—about the issues it raises and the characters who are involved—is one of the most rewarding and pleasurable ways of studying Shakespeare. It makes sense to discuss each scene as it is read, sharing impressions—and perhaps correcting misapprehensions. It can be useful to compare aspects of this play with other fictions—plays, novels, films—or with modern life. A large class can divide into small groups, each with a leader, who can discuss different aspects of a single topic and then report back to the main assembly.

Suggestions

A1   the figure of God's majesty,
His captain, steward, deputy, elect,
Anointed, crowned, planted many years . . .   (4, 1, 125–7)

Monarchy, its privileges and responsibilities, are the key issues of
Richard II. What are *your* views on the subject?

A2   Is revenge ever justified?

A3   Are you patriotic? Can you share any of the sentiments
expressed by John of Gaunt in *Act 2, Scene 1*?

A4   According to Gaunt, the England of his day was 'Dear for her
reputation through the world'. How would you rate the reputation
of England today?

A5   'Finds brotherhood in thee no sharper spur?' (1, 2, 9); 'Were
he twenty times my son/I would appeach him' (5, 2, 100–1). Both
Lancaster and York are reproached for putting king and country
before home and family. Would *you* do the same?

A6   The bay trees in our country are all wither'd
And meteors fright the fixed stars of heaven . . .   (2, 4, 8–9)

The Welsh captain and his soldiers have all been frightened by
these phenomena, interpreting them as portents of disaster. Are
you superstitious? Do you believe in the supernatural?

B   Character Study

Shakespeare is famous for his creation of characters who seem like
real people. We can judge their actions and we can try to
comprehend their thoughts and feelings—just as we criticize and
try to understand the people we know. As the play progresses, we
learn to like or dislike, love or hate, them—just as though they lived
in *our* world.

Characters can be studied *from the outside*, by observing what
they do and listening sensitively to what they say. This is the
scholar's method: the scholar—or any reader—has access to the
entire play, and can see the function of every character within the
whole scheme of that play.

Another approach works *from the inside*, taking a single
character and looking at the action and the other characters from
his/her point of view. This is the way an actor prepares for
performance, creating a personality who can have only a partial

notion of what is going on, and it asks for a student's inventive imagination and creative writing.

The two methods—both useful in different ways—are really complementary to each other. For both of them it can be very helpful to re-frame the character's speeches *in your own words*, using the vocabulary and idiom of everyday parlance.

Suggestions

a) from 'outside' the character

B1 From tyrant to victim, from villain to suffering hero . . . Chart the changes in the role and character of Richard II.

B2 How far would you agree with the view that 'Bullingbrook's righteous indignation is flawed from the very beginning by his overreaching ambition'?

B3 'York has no character of his own: he is an emotional weather-vane pointing the direction of the winds of change.' Do you agree?

B4 'The three female characters are minor triumphs, created to serve the special needs of the dramatist.' How would you describe the personalities and functions of

a) the queen
b) the Duchess of Gloucester
c) the Duchess of York?

B5 Aumerle—Richard's trusted favourite, and his mother's 'old son' (5, 3, 145). Write a detailed character study.

b) from 'inside' the character

B6 Crime and punishment! Bullingbrook, Mowbray, Lancaster, and King Richard have all kept journals recording their thoughts and feelings during the trial at Windsor. Write one of these.

B7 'Death of a Patriot': York describes the death of John of Gaunt

i) to his sister-in-law (the Duchess of Gloucester) or his wife
ii) in an official obituary.

B8 Richard's queen has very little to do in the royal Household— so she writes letters! Devise a selection of these—for example:

    i) to friends and family in France describing the ceremonies
      of *Act 1*

   ii) to her husband in Ireland (remembering that she had
      promised 'To lay aside life-harming heaviness And
      entertain a cheerful disposition', *2, 2, 3–4*)

  iii) to the people of France explaining why she is being sent
      home.

B9 'Right on both sides': York writes the memoirs of a man torn between two monarchs.

B10 In the character of Bushy, Bagot, or Green, give an account of your relationship with the king and your influence over his decisions.

B11 As young Henry Percy, describe your first impressions of Bullingbrook. Has he changed at all since you met him?

B12 'A god on earth thou art!' The Duchess of York tells her best friend about her son's conspiracy and Bullingbrook's generosity.

B13 Bullingbrook tells his followers about his encounter with the York family—and demands action!

B14 Richard appears to have no 'inner life'—even his final speech is addressed to an imaginary listener. But perhaps he writes letters, memoirs—or even poems. Compose some of these.

B15 What are the thoughts of the ordinary people who are caught up in extraordinary events? Write the letters or diaries of any of the following:

    a) a lady attending on the queen
    b) a soldier in Bullingbrook's army who witnessed the king's
       surrender
    c) an assistant gardener
    d) the king's groom
    e) the prison warder.

C　Activities

These can involve two or more students, preferably working *away from* the desk or study-table. They can help students to develop a sense of drama and the dramatic aspects of Shakespeare's play—which was written to be *performed*, not read!

C1 Act the play—or at least part of it! Read the first scene 'straight' before studying the rest of *Act I*—then re-read it. How different are your two readings? Conduct the trial of Mowbray in modern language. Can you stage *Richard II* in modern dress?

C2 Use your own words and phraseology to enact the scene (*Act I*, Scene 2) between the Duchess of Gloucester and John of Gaunt.

C3 Fight to the death! Justice by jousting! Nowadays such a spectacular event would be given full media coverage, with considerable debate about the principles and personalities involved and much speculation about the political manoeuvrings behind the situation. Supply this cover, using the techniques of television, radio, and newspaper—both *The Times* and the *Sun*. Try to get interviews with the leading participants and their supporters; present arguments for and against this way of deciding the issue— and question the Bishop of Carlisle about the Church's attitude; ask the sports reporters for the finer points of jousting techniques, and invite bookmakers to lay odds on the contestants.

C4 'How fares our noble uncle Lancaster?' (*2, I, 71*). Devise a scene in which the queen tells her friends in France about her husband's treatment of the dying Gaunt.

C5 'The king is not himself, but basely led By flatterers' (*2, I, 241–2*). Richard's 'favourites'—Bushy, Bagot, and Green— are never seen in private: provide a scene in which, without fear of being overheard, they discuss the king and their power over him.

C6 What do the soldiers think about their leaders, their strategies, and the progress of their campaigns? Invent scenes of camp-fire gossip for soldiers led by

    i) Bullingbrook, advancing south from Ravenspurgh
    ii) a Welsh Captain, waiting for the king to return from Ireland
    iii) the king himself, in Ireland and Wales.

C7 Whatever happens at Flint Castle could change the English monarchy for ever. All eyes turn to Wales. Send a full outside-broadcast team from television and radio services, and all newspaper reporters. Make sure that there is a good running commentary which detects and interprets every movement. Get all the interviews you can—with York, Northumberland, Aumerle, and the Bishop of Carlisle if possible. Speculate about the likely outcome—what will Bullingbrook do next, what does Richard intend, how will the common people be affected, will taxes rise? Devise headlines; improvise cartoons and compose ballads.

C8 'Come home with me to supper. I will lay A plot shall show us all a merry day' (*4*, *1*, 332–3). Devise and perform a scene in which the Abbot of Westminster reveals his 'plot' to Aumerle and the Bishop of Carlisle.

C9 There is very little comedy in *Richard II*, but Bullingbrook apparently finds some amusement in the Duke and Duchess of York ('Our scene is alter'd from a serious thing, And now chang'd to "The Beggar and the King" ', *5*, *3*, 78–9). Perform this scene, striving for comedy without losing the dignity of the characters. The servant who brings York's boots could be very useful here!

C10 The king is dead—long live the king! All the media respond to the occasion. Prepare a 'Special Issue' newspaper; organize radio/television discussions debating the career of the dead king and speculating on the future of his successor (remembering that Henry IV has an 'unthrifty son' who is likely to become Henry V); devise prayers for the country, the people, the government, and the monarchy. Compose obituaries for King Richard.

D   Context Questions

In written examinations, these questions present you with short passages from the play and ask you to explain them. They are intended to test your knowledge of the play and your understanding of its words. Usually you have to make a choice of passages: there may be five on the paper, and you are asked to choose three. Be very sure that you know exactly how many passages you must choose. Study the ones offered to you, and select those you feel most certain of. Make your answers accurate and concise—don't waste time writing more than the examiner is asking for.

D1   He that hath suffer'd this disorder'd spring
Hath now himself met with the fall of leaf.
The weeds which his broad spreading leaves did shelter,
That seem'd in eating him to hold him up,
Are pluck'd up root and all by———.

(i) Who speaks these lines? To whom is he speaking?
(ii) Who else is listening to him?

(iii) Who are the two people referred to ('He' and '——')?
(iv) What particular 'weeds' is the speaker thinking of?

D2   And speaking it, he wishtly look'd on me
As who should say 'I would thou wert the man
That would divorce this terror from my heart',
Meaning the king at Pomfret. Come, let's go.
I am the king's friend, and will rid his foe.

(i) Who is speaking and who is 'he'?
(ii) Where is 'Pomfret'?
(iii) What does 'he' want the speaker to do?
(iv) Will 'he' praise whatever the speaker does next?

D3   So when this thief, this traitor,——, . . .
Shall see us rising in our throne the east
His treasons will sit blushing in his face,
Not able to endure the sight of day,
But self-affrighted tremble at his sin.
Not all the water in the rough rude sea
Can wash the balm off from an anointed king.

(i) Who is speaking and where has he been?
(ii) Where is the speaker now?
(iii) Who is the 'traitor'?
(iv) What does in fact 'wash off' the balm?

D4   Wrath-kindl'd gentlemen, be rul'd by me.
Let's purge this choler without letting blood.
This we prescribe though no physician.
Deep malice makes too deep incision.
Forget, forgive, conclude and be agreed.
Our doctors say this is no month to bleed.

(i) Who is the speaker and who are the 'gentlemen'?
(ii) Why are the 'gentlemen' angry?
(iii) What is the outcome of this attempt to make peace?
(iv) Who is, finally, the victor?

E   Comprehension and Appreciation Questions

These also present passages from the play and ask questions about them; again you often have a choice of passages. But the extracts are much longer than those presented as context questions. A detailed knowledge of the language of the play is required here, and you must be able to express unusual or archaic phrases in your own

words; you may also be expected to comment critically on the
dramatic techniques of the passage and the poetic effectiveness of
Shakespeare's language.

E1   **York**
            Where did I leave?
                    Duchess
                            At that sad stop, my lord,
            Where rude misgovern'd hands from windows' tops
            Threw dust and rubbish on King Richard's head.
                    York
            Then, as I said, the duke, great Bullingbrook,
            Mounted upon a hot and fiery steed   5
            Which his aspiring rider seem'd to know,
            With slow but stately pace kept on his course,
            Whilst all tongues cried 'God save thee, Bullingbrook!'
            You would have thought the very windows spake,
            So many greedy looks of young and old   10
            Through casements darted their desiring eyes
            Upon his visage, and that all the walls
            With painted imagery had said at once
            'Jesu preserve thee! Welcome, Bullingbrook!'
            Whilst he from one side to the other turning,   15
            Bare headed, lower than his proud steed's neck,
            Bespake them thus: 'I thank you, countrymen',
            And thus still doing, thus he pass'd along.
                    Duchess
            Alack, poor Richard. Where rode he the whilst?
                    York
            As in a theatre the eyes of men   20
            After a well-grac'd actor leaves the stage
            Are idly bent on him that enters next,
            Thinking his prattle to be tedious,
            Even so or with much more contempt men's eyes
            Did scowl on Richard. No man cried 'God save him',   25
            No joyful tongue gave him his welcome home,
            But dust was thrown upon his sacred head,
            Which with such gentle sorrow he shook off,
            His face still combating with tears and smiles,
            The badges of his grief and patience,   30
            That had not God for some strong purpose steel'd
            The hearts of men they must perforce have melted
            And barbarism itself have pitied him.

But heaven hath a hand in these events,
To whose high will we bound our calm contents. 35
To Bullingbrook are we sworn subjects now,
Whose state and honour I for aye allow.

(i) What is the meaning of '*misgovern'd*' (line 2); '*casements*'
(line 11); '*visage*' (line 12); '*well-grac'd*' (line 21); '*badges*'
(line 30)?

(ii) Express in your own words the meaning of lines 9–14,
'You would . . . Bullingbrook'; lines 20–3, 'As in a theatre
. . . tedious'.

(iii) What does this passage show of the character of the Duke
of York?

(iv) Show how this passage is influential in changing our
attitude to King Richard.

E2   **Gaunt**
God's is the quarrel, for God's substitute,
His deputy anointed in His sight,
Hath caus'd his death, the which if wrongfully
Let heaven revenge, for I may never lift
An angry arm against His minister. 5
    Duchess
Where then, alas, may I complain myself?
    Gaunt
To God, the widow's champion and defence.
    Duchess
Why then I will. Farewell, old Gaunt.
Thou goest to Coventry, there to behold
Our cousin Herford and fell Mowbray fight. 10
Oh, set my husband's wrongs on Herford's spear,
That it may enter butcher Mowbray's breast!
Or if misfortune miss the first career
Be Mowbray's sins so heavy in his bosom
That they may break his foaming courser's back, 15
And throw the rider headlong in the lists,
A caitiff recreant to my cousin Herford.
Farewell, old Gaunt. Thy sometime brother's wife
With her companion grief must end her life.
    Gaunt
Sister, farewell. I must to Coventry. 20
As much good stay with thee as go with me.

Duchess

Yet one word more. Grief boundeth where it falls,
Not with the empty hollowness, but weight.
I take my leave before I have begun,
For sorrow ends not when it seemeth done.   25
Commend me to thy brother Edmund York.
Lo, this is all. Nay, yet depart not so;
Though this be all, do not so quickly go.
I shall remember more. Bid him, ah, what!
With all good speed at Plashy visit me.   30
Alack, and what shall good old York there see
But empty lodgings and unfurnish'd walls,
Unpeopled offices, untrodden stones,
And what hear there for welcome but my groans?
Therefore commend me, let him not come there,   35
To seek out sorrow that dwells everywhere.
Desolate, desolate will I hence and die.
The last leave of thee takes my weeping eye.

 (i) What is meant by '*career*' (line 13); '*lists*' (line 16); '*caitiff recreant*' (line 17); '*sometime*' (line 18); '*Commend*' (line 26)?
 (ii) Express in your own words the meaning of line 21, 'As much . . . me'; lines 22–3, 'Grief . . . weight'; lines 32–3, 'empty lodgings . . . stones'.
 (iii) Comment on Shakespeare's use of rhyme in this passage.
 (iv) What is the importance of this episode in the first Act of the play?

F   Essays

These will usually give you a specific topic to discuss, or perhaps a question that must be answered, in writing, *with a reasoned argument*. They *never* want you to tell the story of the play—so don't! Your examiner—or teacher—has read the play, and does not need to be reminded of it. Relevant quotations will always help you to make your points more strongly.

F1 How far would you agree with the son of Mowbray who said (*Henry IV, Part 2, 4, 1, 125–6*) that

> . . . when the king did throw his warder down,
> His own life hung upon the staff he threw?

F2 According to the historian Nigel Saul, Shakespeare saw 'the very essence of Richard's tragedy' in the fact that 'Richard, though unkinged, was still kingly'. Do you agree?

F3 'I cannot believe that Shakespeare looked on his Richard II with any but sympathetic eyes'—W. B. Yeats. Do you share this opinion?

F4   Now is this golden crown like a deep well
That owes two buckets, filling one another,
The emptier ever dancing in the air,
The other down, unseen and full of water   (*4*, 1, 183–6)

Show how the balance of power throughout the play is shifted from one dominant male to another.

F5 Could it be said that Bullingbrook is patriotic where Richard is merely idealistic?

F6 'The female characters in *Richard II* follow their hearts without reservation, but their male counterparts are often held back by the caution of their minds.' Is this true?

G   Projects

In some schools, students are required to do more 'free-ranging' work, which takes them outside the text—but which should always be relevant to the play. Such Projects may demand skills other than reading and writing: design and artwork, for instance, may be involved. Sometimes a 'portfolio' of work is assembled over a considerable period of time; and this can be offered to the examiner for assessment.

The availability of resources will, obviously, do much to determine the nature of the Projects; but this is something that only the local teachers will understand. However, there is always help to be found in libraries, museums, and art galleries.

Suggested Subjects

G1 Images of the King.

G2 Tournaments.

G3 Royal Regalia.

G4 A 'Richard' to remember: great performances of the past.

G5 Staging the play: set designs for *Richard II*.

G6 Dressing the play: costumes for *Richard II*—or for Richard II.

Background

England c. 1595

When Shakespeare was writing *Richard II*, many people still believed that the sun went round the earth. They were taught that this was a divinely ordered scheme of things, and that—in England—God had instituted a Church and ordained a Monarchy for the right government of the land and the populace.

'The past is a foreign country; they do things differently there.'

L. P. Hartley

Government

For most of Shakespeare's life, the reigning monarch of England was Queen Elizabeth I. With her counsellors and ministers, she governed the nation (population about five million) from London, although not more than half a million people inhabited the capital city. In the rest of the country, law and order were maintained by the land-owners and enforced by their deputies. The average man had no vote, and his wife had no rights at all.

Religion

At this time, England was a Christian country. All children were baptized, soon after they were born, into the Church of England; they were taught the essentials of the Christian faith, and instructed in their duty to God and to humankind. Marriages were performed, and funerals conducted, only by the licensed clergy and in accordance with the Church's rites and ceremonies. Attendance at divine service was compulsory; absences (without good—medical—reason) could be punished by fines. By such means, the authorities were able to keep some check on the populace—recording births, marriages, and deaths; being alert to any religious nonconformity, which could be politically dangerous; and ensuring a minimum of orthodox instruction through the official 'Homilies' which were regularly preached from the pulpits of all parish churches throughout the realm.

Following Henry VIII's break away from the Church of Rome, all people in England were able to hear the church services *in their own language*. The Book of Common Prayer was used in every church, and an English translation of the Bible was read aloud in public. The Christian religion had never been so well taught before!

Education

School education reinforced the Church's teaching. From the age of four, boys might attend the 'petty school' (French '*petite école*') to learn the rudiments of reading and writing along with a few prayers; some schools also included work with numbers. At the age of seven, the boy was ready for the grammar school (if his father was willing and able to pay the fees).

Here, a thorough grounding in Latin grammar was followed by translation work and the study of Roman authors, paying attention as much to style as to matter. The arts of fine writing were thus inculcated from early youth. A very few students proceeded to university; these were either clever scholarship boys, or else the sons of noblemen. Girls stayed at home, and acquired domestic and social skills—cooking, sewing, perhaps even music. The lucky ones might learn to read and write.

Language

At the start of the sixteenth century the English had a very poor opinion of their own language: there was little serious writing in English, and hardly any literature. Latin was the language of international scholarship, and Englishmen admired the eloquence of the Romans. They made many translations, and in this way they extended the resources of their own language, increasing its vocabulary and stretching its grammatical structures. French, Italian, and Spanish works were also translated and, for the first time, there were English versions of the Bible. By the end of the century, English was a language to be proud of: it was rich in synonyms, capable of infinite variety and subtlety, and ready for all kinds of word-play—especially the *puns*, for which Elizabethan English is renowned.

Drama

The great art-form of the Elizabethan and Jacobean age was its drama. The Elizabethans inherited a tradition of play-acting from the Middle Ages, and they reinforced this by reading and translating the Roman playwrights. At the beginning of the sixteenth century plays were performed by groups of actors, all-male companies (boys acted the female roles) who travelled from town to town, setting up their stages in open places (such as inn-yards) or, with the permission of the owner, in the hall of some noble house. The touring companies continued in the provinces into the seventeenth century; but in London, in 1576, a new building was erected for the performance of plays. This was the Theatre, the first purpose-built playhouse in England. Other playhouses followed, (including the Globe, where most of Shakespeare's plays were performed), and the English drama reached new heights of eloquence.

There were those who disapproved, of course. The theatres, which brought large crowds together, could encourage the spread of disease—and dangerous ideas. During the summer, when the plague was at its worst, the playhouses were closed. A constant censorship was imposed, more or less severe at different times. The Puritan faction tried to close down the theatres, but—partly because there was royal favour for the drama, and partly because the buildings were outside the city limits—they did not succeed until 1642.

Theatre

From contemporary comments and sketches—most particularly a drawing by a Dutch visitor, Johannes de Witt—it is possible to form some idea of the typical Elizabethan playhouse for which most of Shakespeare's plays were written. Hexagonal in shape, it had three roofed galleries encircling an open courtyard. The plain, high stage projected into the yard, where it was surrounded by the audience of standing 'groundlings'. At the back were two doors for the actors' entrances and exits; and above these doors was a balcony—useful for a musicians' gallery or for the acting of scenes '*above*'. Over the stage was a thatched roof, supported on two pillars, forming a canopy—which seems to have been painted with the sun, moon, and stars for the 'heavens'.

Underneath was space (concealed by curtaining) which could be used by characters ascending and descending through a trap-door in the stage. Costumes and properties were kept backstage, in the 'tiring house'. The actors dressed lavishly, often wearing the secondhand clothes bestowed by rich patrons. Stage properties were important for defining a location, but the dramatist's own words were needed to explain the time of day, since all performances took place in the early afternoon.

Further Reading

Barton, Anne, 'Shakespeare and the Limits of Language', *Shakespeare Survey 24* (1971), 19–30.

Brown, John Russell, *Shakespeare's Plays in Performance* (1966; Penguin Shakespeare Library, 1969).

Brooke, Nicholas (ed.), *'Richard II': a Casebook* (1973).

Ellis Fermor, Una, 'Shakespeare's Political Plays', *The Frontiers of Drama* (London, 1945; reprinted (University Paperbacks), 1964).

Kantorowicz, Ernst H., *The King's Two Bodies: A Study in Medieval Political Theology* (Princeton, 1957).

Palmer, John, *Political Characters of Shakespeare* (1945).

Ribner, Irving, *The English History Play in the Age of Shakespeare* (1957, rev. edn. 1965).

Sprague, Arthur C., *Shakespeare's Histories: Plays for the Stage* (1964).

Tillyard, E. M. W., 'Links between Shakespeare's History Plays', *Studies in Philology* 50 (1953), 168–87.

Sources

Bullough, Geoffrey (ed.), *Narrative and Dramatic Sources of Shakespeare*, vol. 4 (London, 1962).

Muir, Kenneth, *The Sources of Shakespeare's Plays* (London, 1977).

Additional background reading

Blake, N. F., *Shakespeare's Language: an Introduction*, (London, 1983).

Muir, K., and Schoenbaum, S., *A New Companion to Shakespeare Studies* (Cambridge, 1971).

Schoenbaum, S., *William Shakespeare: A Documentary Life* (Oxford, 1975).

Thomson, Peter, *Shakespeare's Theatre* (London, 1983).

William Shakespeare, 1564–1616

Elizabeth I was Queen of England when Shakespeare was born in 1564. He was the son of a tradesman who made and sold gloves in the small town of Stratford-upon-Avon, and he was educated at the grammar school in that town. Shakespeare did not go to university when he left school, but worked, perhaps in his father's business. When he was eighteen he married Anne Hathaway, who became the mother of his daughter, Susanna, in 1583, and of twins in 1585.

There is nothing exciting, or even unusual, in this story; and from 1585 until 1592 there are no documents that can tell us anything at all about Shakespeare. But we have learned that in 1592 he was known in London, and that he had become both an actor and a playwright.

We do not know when Shakespeare wrote his first play, and indeed we are not sure of the order in which he wrote his works. If you look on page 135 at the list of his writings and their approximate dates, you will see how he started by writing plays on subjects taken from the history of England. No doubt this was partly because he was always an intensely patriotic man—but he was also a very shrewd business-man. He could see that the theatre audiences enjoyed being shown their own history, and it was certain that he would make a profit from this kind of drama.

The plays in the next group are mainly comedies, with romantic love-stories of young people who fall in love with one another, and at the end of the play marry and live happily ever after.

At the end of the sixteenth century the happiness disappears, and Shakespeare's plays become melancholy, bitter, and tragic. This change may have been caused by some sadness in the writer's life (one of his twins died in 1596). Shakespeare, however, was not the only writer whose works at this time were very serious. The whole of England was facing a crisis. Queen Elizabeth I was growing old. She was greatly loved, and the people were sad to think she must soon die; they were also afraid, for the queen had never married, and so there was no child to succeed her.

When James I came to the throne in 1603, Shakespeare continued to write serious drama—the great tragedies and the plays based on Roman history (such as *Julius Caesar*) for which he is most famous. Finally, before he retired from the theatre, he wrote another set of comedies. These all have the same theme: they tell of happiness which is lost, and then found again.

Shakespeare returned from London to Stratford, his home town. He was rich and successful, and he owned one of the biggest houses in the town. He died in 1616.

Shakespeare also wrote two long poems, and a collection of sonnets. The sonnets describe two love-affairs, but we do not know who the lovers were. Although there are many public documents concerned with his career as a writer and a business-man, Shakespeare has hidden his personal life from us. A nineteenth-century poet, Matthew Arnold, addressed Shakespeare in a poem, and wrote, 'We ask and ask—Thou smilest, and art still'.

There is not even a trustworthy portrait of the world's greatest dramatist.

Approximate order of composition of Shakespeare's works

Period	Comedies	History plays	Tragedies	Poems
I	Comedy of Errors	Henry VI, part 1	Titus Andronicus	
	Taming of the Shrew	Henry VI, part 2		
1594	Two Gentlemen of Verona	Henry VI, part 3		Venus and Adonis
		Richard III		Rape of Lucrece
	Love's Labour's Lost	King John		
II	Midsummer Night's Dream	Richard II	Romeo and Juliet	Sonnets
	Merchant of Venice	Henry IV, part 1		
1599	Merry Wives of Windsor	Henry IV, part 2		
	Much Ado About Nothing			
	As You Like It	Henry V		
III	Twelfth Night		Julius Caesar	
	Troilus and Cressida		Hamlet	
1608	Measure for Measure		Othello	
	All's Well That Ends Well		Timon of Athens	
			King Lear	
			Macbeth	
			Antony and Cleopatra	
			Coriolanus	
IV	Pericles			
1613	Cymbeline	Henry VIII		
	The Winter's Tale			
	The Tempest			